SINGER

SEWING REFERENCE LIBRARY®

Sewing Pants That Fit

Cy DeCosse Incorporated
Minnetonka, Minnesota

SINGER

SEWING REFERENCE LIBRARY®

Sewing Pants That Fit

Contents

Copyright © 1989
Cy DeCosse Incorporated
5900 Green Oak Drive
Minnetonka, Minnesota 55343
1-800-328-3895
All rights reserved
Printed in U.S.A.

Also available from the publisher: *Sewing
Essentials, Sewing for the Home, Clothing Care
& Repair, Sewing for Style, Sewing Specialty
Fabrics, Sewing Activewear, The Perfect Fit,
Timesaving Sewing, More Sewing for the Home,
Tailoring, Sewing for Children, Sewing Update
No. 1, Sewing Update No. 2, Sewing with an
Overlock, 101 Sewing Secrets*

Library of Congress
Cataloging-in-Publication Data

Sewing Pants That Fit

 p.cm. — (Singer sewing reference library)
ISBN 0-86573-251-5
ISBN 0-86573-252-3 (pbk.)
1. Trousers. 2. Machine sewing. I. Series.
TT542.S48 1989   89-37405
646.4'3304 — dc20   CIP

Distributed by: Contemporary Books, Inc.
 Chicago, Illinois

CY DE COSSE INCORPORATED
Chairman: Cy DeCosse
President: James B. Maus
Executive Vice President: William B. Jones

SEWING PANTS THAT FIT
Created by: The Editors of Cy DeCosse
 Incorporated, in cooperation with the
 Sewing Education Department, Singer
 Sewing Company. Singer is a trademark
 of The Singer Company and is used
 under license.
Executive Editor: Zoe Graul
Technical Director: Rita C. Opseth
Project Manager: Ann Schlachter
Senior Art Director: Rebecca Gammelgaard

Writer: Phyllis Galbraith
Editors: Janice Cauley, Bernice Maehren
Sample Coordinators: Wendy Fedie, Joanne Wawra
Technical Photo Director: Bridget Haugh
Sewing Staff: Phyllis Galbraith, Bridget Haugh, Sara Holmen, Linda Neubauer, Carol Olson, Lori Ritter, Nancy Sundeen, John Willcox
Fabric Editors: Marie Castle, Wendy Fedie, Joanne Wawra
Photo Studio Manager: Cathleen Shannon

Photographers: Bobbette Destiche, Rex Irmen, Tony Kubat, John Lauenstein, Bill Lindner, Mark Macemon, Charles Nields, Mette Nielsen
Production Manager: Jim Bindas
Assistant Production Managers: Julie Churchill, Amelia Merz
Production Staff: Russell Beaver, Holly Clements, Sheila DiPaola, Joe Fahey, Kevin D. Frakes, Yelena Konrardy, Scott Lamoureux, Jody Phillips, Linda Schloegel, Greg Wallace, Nik Wogstad

Consultants: Sandra Betzina, Janet Hethorn, Marcy Tilton
Contributers: Anglo Fabrics Company, Inc.; Burda Patterns Inc.; Coats & Clark Inc.; EZ International; Hamilton Adams Imports Ltd.; Kwik-Sew® Pattern Co., Inc.; Landau Woolen Co. Inc.; The McCall Pattern Co.; Minnetonka Mills, Inc.; Pellon Division/Freudenberg NonWovens; Simplicity Pattern Co. Inc.; Singer Sewing Company, Solar-Kist Corp.; Woolmark Inc., Vogue/Butterick Patterns
Color Separations: Scantrans
Printing: Ringier America, Inc. (1089)

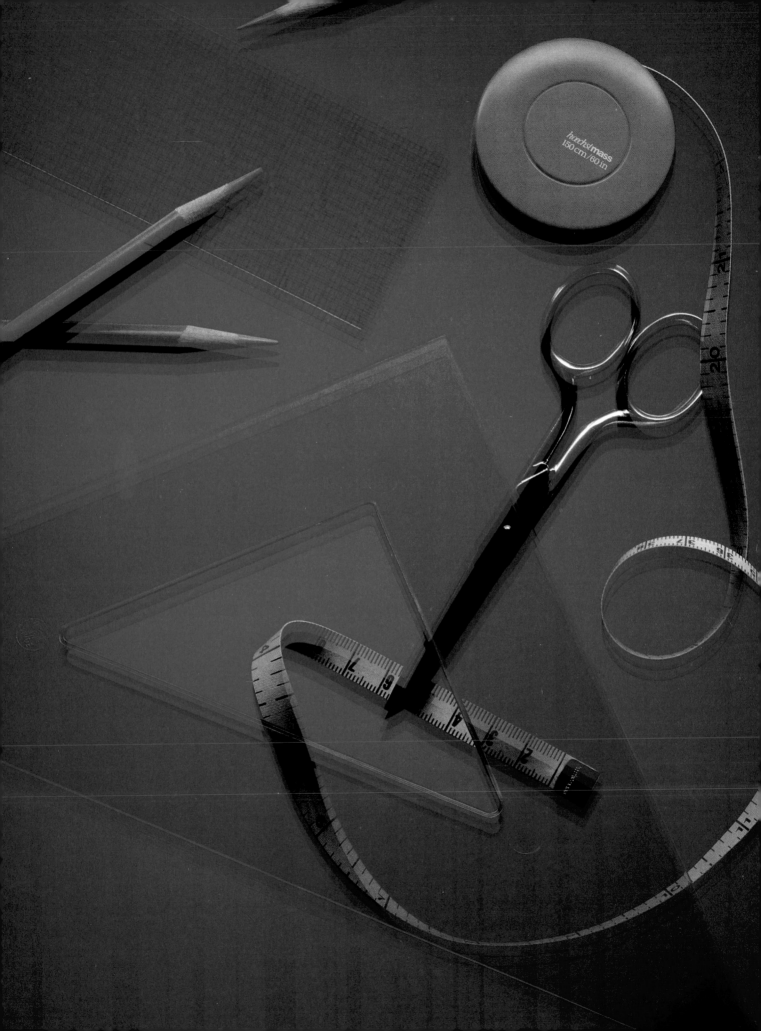

How to Use This Book

Patterns are available for sewing pants in any number of different styles, and with the wide range of suitable pants fabrics, the variety of looks is almost unlimited. *Sewing Pants That Fit* helps you select your pattern and fabric and takes you through the process of fitting and sewing pants, step-by-step. Even though, in the past, you may have had difficulty fitting pants, do not let this discourage you. If you follow the methods in this book and take them one step at a time, the fitting process is not difficult.

Understanding Fit

The main goal when fitting pants is for the person wearing them to be pleased with their final appearance and to be comfortable. To sew pants that fit, you must first understand what good fit is; use the Standards of Fit charts provided in this book as a guideline for achieving good fit.

The Understanding Fit section of the book illustrates how pants patterns are shaped to correspond to the body. Analyze your body by taking measurements and looking at yourself in the mirror as objectively as possible. Use the photographs of poor-fitting pants in this section to help identify your fitting problems.

Pattern & Fitting Adjustments

Although you may have avoided pattern adjustments in the past, they are an important step in sewing pants that fit. You will not need all the adjustments in the Pattern Adjustments section, but it will be helpful for you to read through the entire section to gain a better understanding of fitting pants.

You will be shown how to mark adjustment lines on the pattern. The pattern is then adjusted along these lines to avoid distorting the pattern shape or design.

When you adjust the pattern, the seamlines are broken and may jog in the adjustment areas. It is then necessary to redraw, or true, them for smooth seamlines. It is recommended that you add wider seam

allowances to the pattern for the first pants you sew, to allow extra room for any fitting adjustments that may be needed.

After pattern adjustments are made, cut and machine-baste the pants, and try them on to check the fit. The Perfecting the Fit section shows you the correct sequence for checking the fit of the pants and how to make any minor adjustments that may be needed. If any adjustments are made on the basted pants, the adjustments should then be transferred to the pattern.

Constructing the Pants

You will learn special sewing techniques in the Constructing the Pants section, including how to sew slant pockets that are stabilized to prevent the opening from stretching and how to sew a fly-front zipper with a fly shield. You will also learn special techniques for pressing creases and for pressing smooth seams, darts, and pleats.

There is information on using two closures, a main closure and a secondary closure, to distribute the stress and prevent pulling at the top of the zipper.

Learn how to cut lining fabric for fully lined pants by using the adjusted pattern pieces, and how to partially line pants in the knee area.

Design Variations

The Design Variations section shows you how to change the look of a basic pattern by adding a watch pocket. By using simple flat pattern methods, you can change the width of the pants legs, change a dart-fitted pants pattern to a pleated pants pattern, or add cuffs.

This section also includes special techniques for pull-on pants, such as how to sew one-piece pockets and how to apply an elasticized waistband.

Selections

Sewing Pants

By making your own pants, you can have pants that fit perfectly. And with so many patterns and fabrics to choose from, there is a perfect style for everyone.

The length of pants varies greatly from one style to another; lengths, ranging from the upper thigh to the ankle bone, include short shorts, Jamaica shorts, Bermuda shorts, walking shorts, knickers, pedal pushers, Capri pants, and classic pants.

Pull-on pants have an elasticized waistband instead of a placket. They are easy to sew and comfortable to wear.

Classic pants are a good choice for the first pair of pants you sew. After you adjust this basic pants pattern to fit, it is easier to adjust other styles.

Bermuda shorts are shorts that end just above the knee.

Culottes are pants that are cut fuller to resemble a skirt.

Capri pants end above the ankle and are cut slender for a trim look.

Jodhpurs are riding pants that flare at the thighs and have narrow straight-cut legs below the knee.

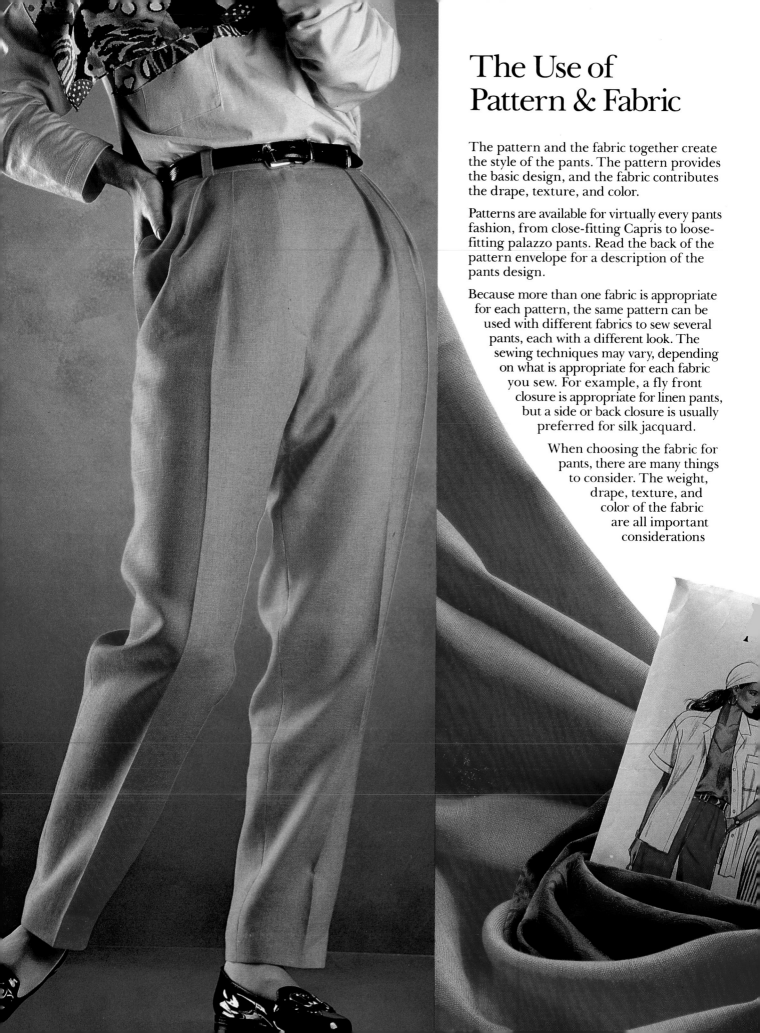

The Use of Pattern & Fabric

The pattern and the fabric together create the style of the pants. The pattern provides the basic design, and the fabric contributes the drape, texture, and color.

Patterns are available for virtually every pants fashion, from close-fitting Capris to loose-fitting palazzo pants. Read the back of the pattern envelope for a description of the pants design.

Because more than one fabric is appropriate for each pattern, the same pattern can be used with different fabrics to sew several pants, each with a different look. The sewing techniques may vary, depending on what is appropriate for each fabric you sew. For example, a fly front closure is appropriate for linen pants, but a side or back closure is usually preferred for silk jacquard.

When choosing the fabric for pants, there are many things to consider. The weight, drape, texture, and color of the fabric are all important considerations that affect the hang and appearance of the finished pants. If the pants pattern has special design details, such as pockets or yokes, it is also important to select a fabric that will enhance the details (pages 14 and 15).

Also consider the activities for which the pants will be worn. For example, if the pants are for activewear, you should select a durable fabric, but if the pants are for evening wear, durability is not as important.

If wrinkles are objectionable to you, check the fabric by crushing it to see how easily it wrinkles. Keep in mind that pants that fit well do not wrinkle as much as pants that fit poorly.

Check the drape of the fabric against the body while standing in front of the mirror. Bulky or stiff fabric stands away from the body, while lightweight or supple fabric falls closer to the body and drapes in soft folds. If you are sewing pleated pants, fold pleats in the fabric to see how they will drape.

NLOOK
6865

Selecting Fabrics

The fabric you choose should enhance the design details of the pants. For example, if you are sewing pants with creases or details that require crisp edges, choose a sturdy fabric that will hold a sharp press. For pants with soft gathers, choose a lighter-weight fabric that drapes softly.

The lightness or darkness of the fabric color is an important consideration if the pants pattern has special design details; details are more noticeable on pants in medium-value colors than on pants in dark colors. Details also show up better on solid-color fabrics than on patterned fabrics, such as prints or plaids. Even textured fabrics, such as tweeds, can make details less noticeable.

If you want to emphasize the silhouette of the pants, select a fabric in a dark color, even though the design details will not show up as well.

Fabrics with vertical stripes emphasize the vertical line of pants, but wide stripes make you look heavier than narrow stripes. This is even more noticeable with wide stripes of strongly contrasting colors.

When selecting a striped, plaid, or print fabric for pants, hold the fabric up to you in front of a mirror to check the effect. A small plaid or print may recede, especially if the colors are muted or subtle. A large plaid or print may appear more bold and striking, especially if the colors contrast strongly.

Medium-value solid colors enhance design details and make them more noticeable.

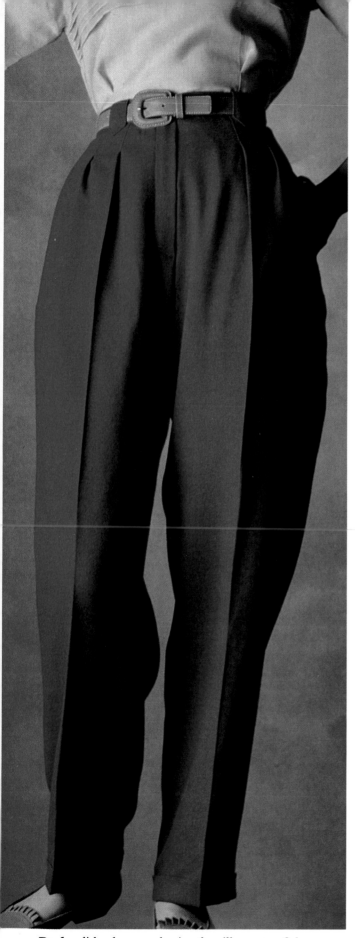

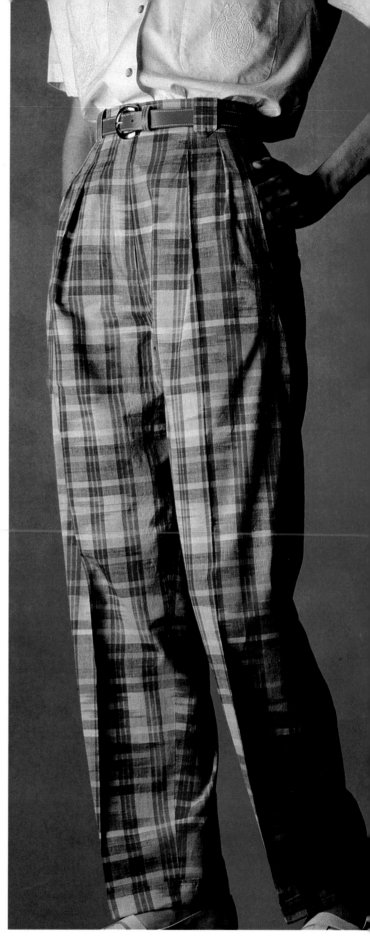

Dark solid colors emphasize the silhouette of the pants and make design details less noticeable.

Patterned fabrics, such as plaids and prints, make design details less noticeable.

Types of Pants Fabric

Fabrics made from natural fibers are good for sewing pants, because they breathe, making the pants more comfortable to wear; they also shape and press well. Natural fibers are frequently blended with synthetic fibers to create fabrics that are more durable and wrinkle-resistant.

A fabric with excellent drapability falls close to the body in soft folds; a fabric with moderate drapability stands away from the body. There are sometimes several weights available in one category of fabric; the lighter in weight a fabric is, the better it drapes. Although most linens, for example, have only moderate drapability, a lightweight linen is more drapable than a heavyweight linen.

Fabrics that tend to stand away from the body may add bulk, causing you to look heavier than you really are; heavier fabrics also add bulk.

Selecting Lining

For lined pants, select a lightweight, smooth lining with a tight weave. The care method for the lining should be compatible with that for the pants fabric.

Bemberg™ rayon breathes well, is comfortable in all climates, and is durable. It is available in two weights; the lighter weight works best for pants.

Silk lining, such as China silk, is less durable than rayon lining, but it also breathes well. Silk is especially suitable for cold-weather climates, and drapes well.

Polyester lining is more readily available but does not drape as well as rayon or silk. Polyester also does not breathe well, making it less comfortable in hot or cold weather.

Guide for Selecting & Sewing Pants Fabric

Lightweight wool flannel, shown (soft fabric with brushed surface); **wool tweed** (fabric with textured surface)

Characteristics: Moderate drapability; adds some bulk; holds crease; does not hold shape well.

Sewing Tips: Avoid overpressing, because fabric may become matted; creases and needle-marks may be removed with steam; lining recommended.

Rayon gabardine (soft, lightweight fabric with twill weave)

Characteristics: Excellent drapability; does not add bulk; may not hold crease.

Sewing Tips: Creases and needle-marks may be removed with steam; allow steamed fabric to dry before moving, to prevent stretching; lining optional.

(continued on next page)

Wool gabardine, shown, **other worsted wools** (tightly woven fabric with hard surface)

Characteristics: Good drapability; does not add bulk if lightweight; holds crease; holds shape well.

Sewing Tips: Avoid overpressing, because fabric may become shiny; use steam and clapper for a sharp press; creases and needle-marks may be removed with steam; lining optional.

Wool crepe (fabric with crimped surface effect)

Characteristics: Excellent drapability; holds crease; does not hold shape well.

Sewing Tips: Preshrinking before cutting is essential; finish raw edges before construction to prevent raveling; creases and needle-marks may be removed with steam; lining recommended.

Wool challis, shown, **rayon challis** (soft, supple, lightweight fabric with smooth surface)

Characteristics: Excellent drapability; does not add bulk; may not hold crease.

Sewing Tips: May need to finish raw edges before construction to prevent raveling; creases and needle-marks may be removed with steam; lining recommended for tailored styles.

Guide for Selecting & Sewing Pants Fabric (continued)

Silk or silklike jacquard, shown, **crepe de chine, charmeuse, broadcloth, other silkies** (lightweight smooth fabrics)

Characteristics: Excellent drapability, especially silk fabrics; holds crease; does not add bulk.

Sewing Tips: May allow more ease when sewing tailored styles; use taut sewing to prevent puckering; creases and needle-marks are difficult to remove; lining optional.

Silk tweed, shown (soft, mediumweight, multicolored fabric with textured surface); **silk noil** (soft, lightweight fabric with nubby texture)

Characteristics: Good drapability; silk tweed adds some bulk; does not hold crease; does not hold shape well.

Sewing Tips: Finish raw edges of silk tweed before construction to prevent raveling; creases and needle-marks may be removed with steam; lining recommended for tailored styles.

Linen suiting (crisp, mediumweight fabric with slubbed texture)

Characteristics: Moderate drapability; adds some bulk; holds crease; wrinkles easily.

Sewing Tips: Finish raw edges before construction to prevent raveling; creases and needle-marks may be removed with steam; lining recommended.

Wool jersey, shown, **cotton knits** (lightweight knit fabrics)

Characteristics: Good drapability; not durable; does not hold crease; does not hold shape well.

Sewing Tips: Stabilize crotch seam with seam tape to prevent stretching; may line pants in knee area only, to prevent bagging.

Silk shantung, shown, **or dupioni** (lightweight fabric with slubbed texture); **silk tussah** (natural-colored fabric with heavily textured, slubbed surface)

Characteristics: Good to moderate drapability; may add some bulk; holds crease.

Sewing Tips: Finish raw edges before construction to prevent raveling; creases and needle-marks are difficult to remove; lining recommended.

Cotton twill, shown, **chino, damask, poplin, denim** (firmly woven, sturdy fabrics)

Characteristics: Moderate drapability; durable; may add bulk, depending on weight of fabric; does not hold crease; does not hold shape well.

Sewing Tips: Preshrinking fabric before cutting helps soften fabric; pants made from these fabrics are usually not lined.

The First Pants You Sew

Although there are many patterns and fabrics to choose from, it is helpful to keep the pattern and fabric simple for the first pants you sew. The fitting process is a significant part of sewing your first pair of pants, so you may want to save time by avoiding patterns that have time-consuming details, such as welt pockets, or fabrics that are challenging to sew.

Pattern Selection

The patterns from each pattern company are based on the fit of that company's dart-fitted pattern, or sloper. Once you have adjusted the dart-fitted pattern, it can be used as a guide for fitting other patterns from the same company. If you intend to make several pants in a variety of styles, the dart-fitted pants pattern is the best choice for your first pants.

Each pattern company also has a classic pleated pants pattern. The fit of the classic pants, below, is usually similar to the fit of the dart-fitted pants, because the classic pants have a minimum amount of design ease. If you do not want to use the dart-fitted pattern for the first pair of pants you sew, the classic pleated pants pattern is a good alternative.

Simple design changes, such as adding cuffs or changing the width of the pants legs or the depth of the pleats (pages 116 to 120), can then be made on a classic pleated pants pattern to create different looks.

The size chart may vary from one pattern company to another; a size 10 pattern, for example, may be designed for a 34½" (87.8 cm) hip measurement by one company and for a 35½" (90.3 cm) hip measurement by another. Be sure to check your body measurements with the sizing chart before selecting the pattern.

The amount of ease allowed in a pattern is determined by comparing the pattern measurement at the hipline to your hip measurement.

Waistband lies at the natural waistline.

Darts provide fitting ease.

Shallow pleats, which are pinned out during the fitting, provide a smooth fit.

Slant pockets or side-seam pockets may be included, if desired.

The ease in a basic pattern may vary from one company to another. Some companies allow 1" to 2" (2.5 to 5 cm) of ease, which gives a smooth fit without excess fullness; others allow up to 3" to 4" (7.5 to 10 cm).

As a general rule, select your pattern size according to your hip measurement. However, if you are sewing a pattern that allows 3" to 4" (7.5 to 10 cm) of ease and you want a closer fit in pants, select a pattern one size smaller to avoid making so many pattern adjustments. If you are uncertain about which pattern size to choose, you may want to buy a multisize pattern.

Fabric Selection

When you sew your first pants, it is important to use a firmly woven, mediumweight fabric that is appropriate for the style. Even the first pants you sew will fit well, so it is not necessary to make a muslin or gingham test garment.

Fabrics made from natural fibers are easy to work with, because they press and shape well. Good choices include wool flannel (1), wool worsted (2), silk tweed (3), linen suiting (4), and cotton twill (5). Avoid loosely woven fabric, because it may stretch out of shape during the fittings.

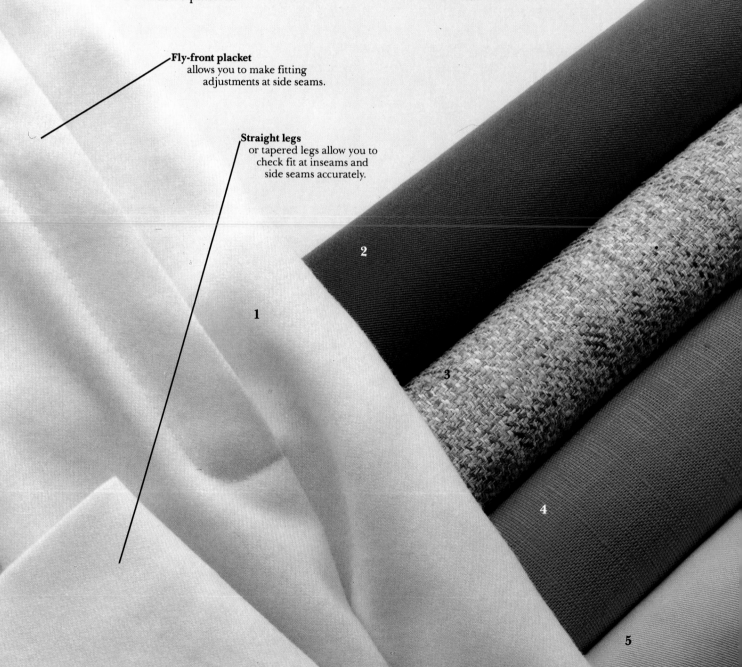

Fly-front placket allows you to make fitting adjustments at side seams.

Straight legs or tapered legs allow you to check fit at inseams and side seams accurately.

Understanding Fit

Fitting Pants

Pattern companies develop sizing charts for a variety of figure types, but few people fit these standards exactly. This means that, in order to get a good fit, you will have to make some adjustments on the pattern. This can be frustrating, but once you have adjusted one pattern, these adjustments can be applied to other patterns from the same company, without going through the whole process again.

The pants are cut from the adjusted pattern, machine-basted together, and tried on for a fitting. Any additional minor adjustments are made at this time. Once the pattern and fitting adjustments are made, constructing the pants is easy.

Basic Ease & Design Ease

All patterns are designed to fit the body's measurements plus ease. *Basic ease* is just enough additional fullness to allow for movement, comfort, and smooth fit. *Design ease* is the amount of fullness added for design, as in pleats, and may change according to the style of the pattern or the current fashion. Whether added for comfort or for appearance, ease ensures a well-fitted, attractive garment.

The pants on the left are an example of basic ease. There is just enough ease for movement, comfort, and smooth fit. The extra fullness created by the pleats in the pants on the right is an example of design ease.

What Is Good Fit?

When you wear pants that fit properly, you should be comfortable whether you are standing, sitting, walking, or bending. When pants are worn, there should not be any wrinkles caused by pulling, or folds from excess fabric.

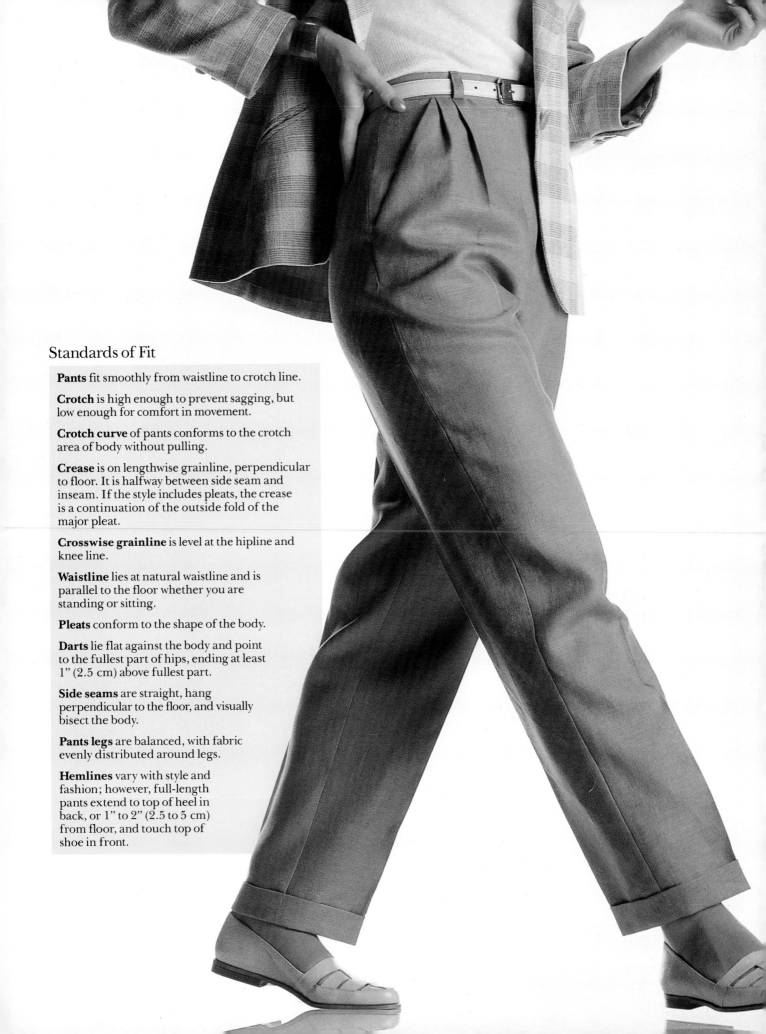

Standards of Fit

Pants fit smoothly from waistline to crotch line.

Crotch is high enough to prevent sagging, but low enough for comfort in movement.

Crotch curve of pants conforms to the crotch area of body without pulling.

Crease is on lengthwise grainline, perpendicular to floor. It is halfway between side seam and inseam. If the style includes pleats, the crease is a continuation of the outside fold of the major pleat.

Crosswise grainline is level at the hipline and knee line.

Waistline lies at natural waistline and is parallel to the floor whether you are standing or sitting.

Pleats conform to the shape of the body.

Darts lie flat against the body and point to the fullest part of hips, ending at least 1" (2.5 cm) above fullest part.

Side seams are straight, hang perpendicular to the floor, and visually bisect the body.

Pants legs are balanced, with fabric evenly distributed around legs.

Hemlines vary with style and fashion; however, full-length pants extend to top of heel in back, or 1" to 2" (2.5 to 5 cm) from floor, and touch top of shoe in front.

Relating the Pattern to the Body

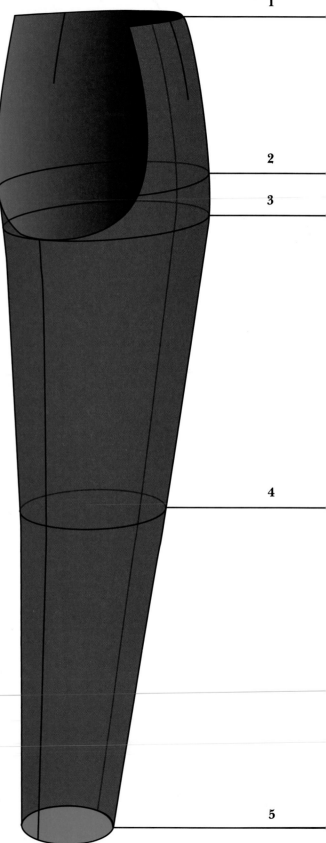

Sewing pants that fit is easier when you understand how the pattern relates to the body. The pattern has straight and curved lines that correspond to the lines of the body. The measurements, or dimensions, of the pattern equal the body measurements, plus ease for movement and design. Adjusting the pants pattern is a matter of adding or subtracting space for each area that differs from the body measurements plus ease. Think of a pattern as a two-dimensional map of your three-dimensional body.

1) Waistline on pattern, with darts or pleats folded out, corresponds to natural waistline of body.

2) Hipline on pattern corresponds to fullest part of hips on body, as viewed from the side.

3) Crotch line on pattern corresponds to the crotch on body.

4) Knee line on pattern corresponds to knee on body.

5) Hemline on pattern corresponds to desired location on body, depending on style of pants.

6) Side seamline on pattern front from waistline to crotch line corresponds to crotch depth measurement of body.

7) Darts and pleats at top of pattern fit waist and high hip of body.

8) Front crotch seamline on pattern from waistline to crotch curve corresponds to angle of body from waist to hipline; seamline is straight in this area.

9) Crotch curve on pattern corresponds to curve of body in crotch area; crotch seam curves at front and back and is straight in between.

10) Back crotch seamline on pattern from waistline to crotch curve corresponds to angle of body from waist to fullest part of seat; seamline is straight in this area.

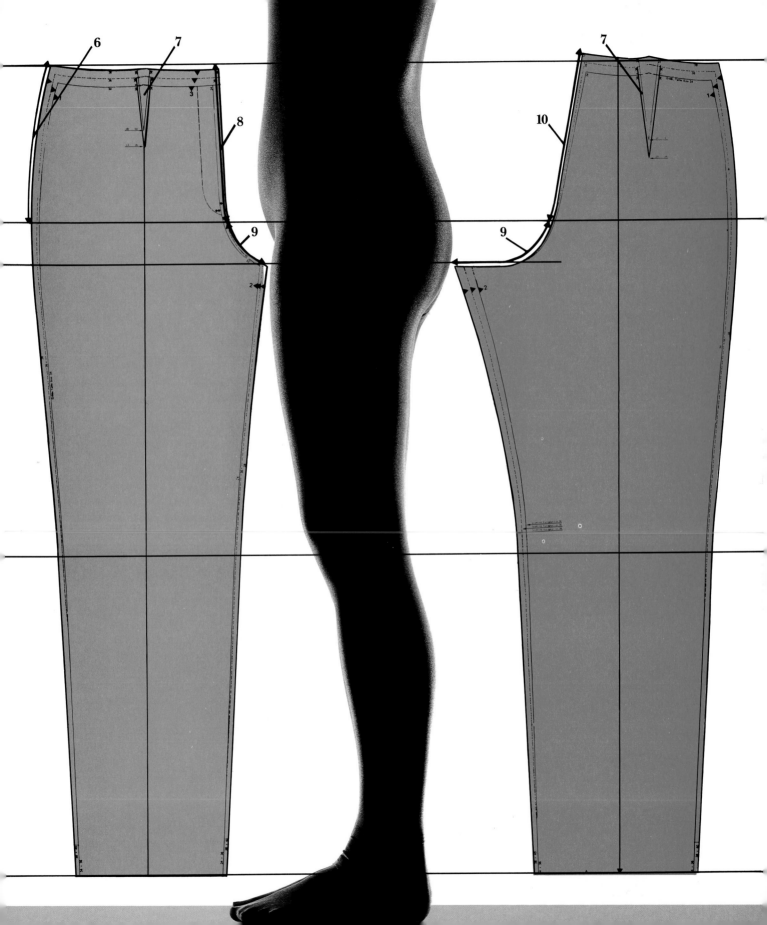

Taking Measurements

Measurements should be taken over the undergarments that you usually wear. Tie narrow elastic or a cord around your waist as a mark from which to measure; if necessary, bend sideways to determine your natural waistline. The cord should be snug, but not pinching. Stand with your weight evenly distributed on both feet. Relax and assume your normal posture.

It is important to take accurate measurements, so it is helpful to have a friend assist you. For accuracy, use a tape measure that is not frayed or stretched. Record your measurements on the Pants Adjustment Chart (pages 30 and 31), and compare your measurements to the pattern measurements to determine where you need to make adjustments on your pattern.

The horizontal measurements are waist and hip circumferences. For these measurements, keep the tape measure snug and parallel to the floor.

The vertical measurements are crotch depth, crotch length, hip depth, waist to knee, and waist to ankle. For these measurements, keep the tape measure snug and perpendicular to the floor.

Taking Horizontal Measurements

Waist circumference. Measure body at natural waist, as marked by elastic.

Hip circumference. Measure body at fullest part of hips, as viewed from side; this is the point where the seat is the fullest. Mark with tape.

Taking Vertical Measurements

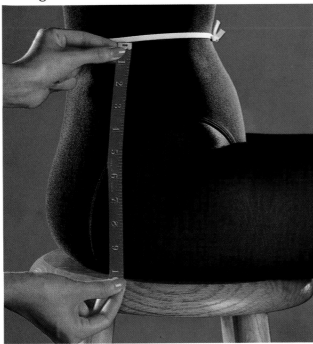

Crotch depth. Sit straight on flat surface, such as table or chair without any indentation or padding; keep knees bent at right angle. At side, measure from elastic, following curve of body to hip, then straight down to surface.

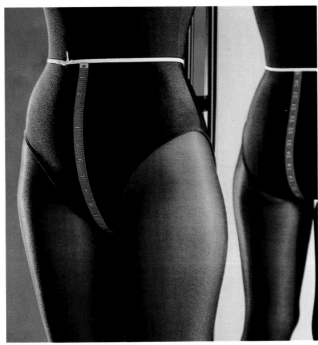

Crotch length. Place end of tape measure at waist at center front; measure between legs and back up to waist at center back. This measurement should be snug against body.

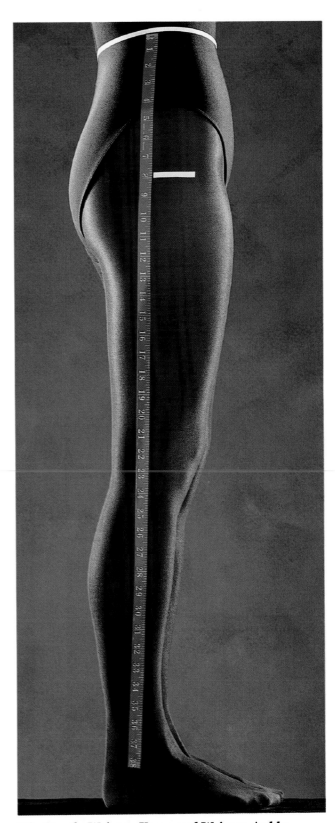

Hip Depth, Waist to Knee, and Waist to Ankle. Measure hip depth at side of body, from bottom of elastic to point where hip circumference was measured. Continue down side to center of knee for waist to knee measurement, and to just below ankle bone for waist to ankle measurement.

Pants Adjustment Chart

To determine the adjustments you need to make on your pattern, begin by recording your "Body Measurements" on the chart, below. (You may want to copy this chart, rather than write in the book.)

Then add the amount of "Ease Needed" to the "Body Measurement" to determine the "Body Measurement Plus Ease." Select the smaller amount of ease from the range recommended if you prefer a closer fit, or the larger amount if you prefer a looser fit.

The "Pattern Measurements" and "Adjustments Needed" are recorded during the pattern adjustment process (pages 50 to 59).

Analyze your body shape and compare your body to the standard figure type, shown opposite; sketch or note any variations between your body and the standard figure type on the front view and side view diagrams.

Fill out the form at right with the appropriate name, date, and pattern. Then record any fitting problems you have had previously. The information on these two pages will give you a complete record for future use.

Pants Adjustment Chart

	Crotch Depth	Waist to Knee	Waist to Ankle	Waist Circumference	
Body Measurement					
Ease Needed	½" (1.3 cm) if hips are less than 37" (94 cm) ¾" (2 cm) if hips are 37" to 40" (94 to 102 cm) 1" (2.5 cm) if hips are 40" (102 cm) or more	no ease needed	no ease needed	1" to 2" (2.5 to 5 cm)	
Body Measurement Plus Ease					
Pattern Measurement					
Adjustment Needed					

Name _____

Date _____

Pattern _____

Fitting Problems _____

_____

_____

_____

_____

_____

_____

_____

_____

_____

_____

_____

Standard Figure Type

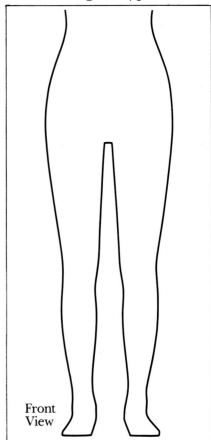

Front View

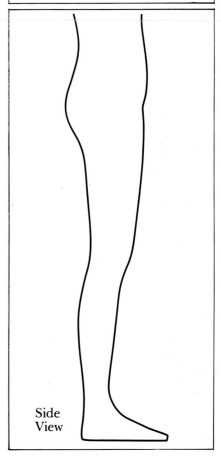

Side View

Hip Circumference	Hip Depth	Crotch Length
1" to 2" (2.5 to 5 cm)	no ease needed	1" (2.5 cm) if hips are less than 37" (94 cm)
		1½" (3.8 cm) if hips are 37" to 40" (94 to 102 cm)
		2" (5 cm) if hips are 40" (102 cm) or more

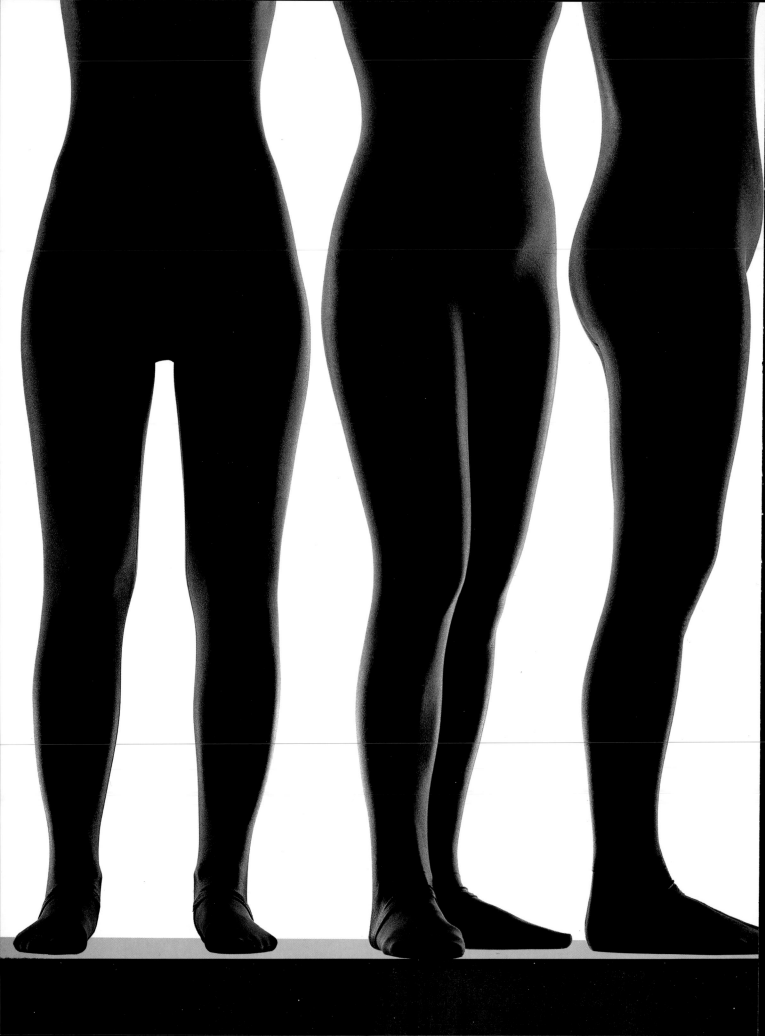

Analyzing Your Figure

Your body measurements tell only a part of the story. The same pants may fit differently on two bodies with identical measurements. Your posture can also affect the way your pants fit. Many fitting problems are the result of posture variations like those below: a backward hip tilt, sometimes called swayback, or a forward hip tilt. A detailed analysis of your body is necessary to provide important information you will need in addition to your measurements.

To make this analysis, stand in front of a mirror, wearing undergarments only, and study the general outline of your body from the front and the side. Use the questions, right, to help you analyze your figure. Sketch or note your observations on page 31.

This step is important if you are to fully understand how your body contours relate to the shape of your pattern. The more objective you can be, the more your observations will help you develop a pants pattern that truly reflects your body form and ensures a good fit. Good fit is always more flattering than wrinkles and folds that point to problem areas.

The pants you now own, whether purchased or sewn from a pattern, can help you discover how your figure varies from the standard figure type (page 31). Ask yourself which fitting problems you encounter most often.

Pages 34 to 42 give examples of common fitting problems and what pattern adjustments are needed to correct them. Read through all the examples, to better understand the relationship between pattern shape and pants fit.

Identifying the problem is the first step in correcting it. Keep in mind that you may have a combination of fitting problems, requiring more than one adjustment. When you identify your fitting problems, take note of the adjustment needed.

Questions to Help Analyze Your Figure

Front View

Is your waist quite a bit narrower than your hips, or are they almost the same width?

Is the fullest part of your hips higher or lower than standard?

Are your thighs fuller than the fullest part of your hips?

Are your legs straight when you stand comfortably, with your weight distributed evenly? Or do they bow out from the knees down, or bend toward each other?

Is one hip higher than the other, or is your hipline parallel to the floor? If one hip looks significantly higher, you may want to take the hip depth and crotch depth measurements for both sides.

Side View

Is your abdomen prominent? If so, how high or low is the fullest part of your abdomen?

Is your seat fairly flat, or does it protrude? How high or low is the fullest part?

Do your hips tilt forward or backward? How do your hips line up in relation to an imaginary plumb line drawn from the side of your waist to the floor?

Analyze Your Posture

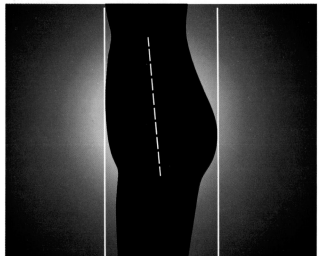

Backward hip tilt. Check for protruding seat if you have backward hip tilt.

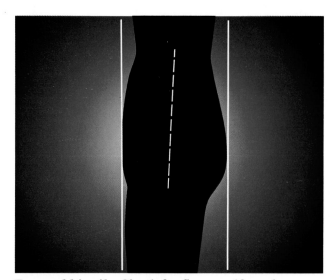

Forward hip tilt. Check for flat seat, if you have forward hip tilt. You may also have protruding front thighs, or prominent abdomen.

Short Crotch Depth

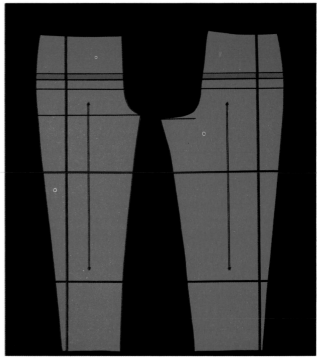

Problem. The distance from waistline to crotch is shorter than standard, causing pants to hang too low in crotch area. Pants are baggy and excess folds may form just below crotch.

Adjustment. Shorten the front and back pattern pieces an equal amount above hipline (page 52).

Long Crotch Depth

Problem. The distance from waistline to crotch is longer than standard, causing pants to pull in crotch area. Wrinkles may form, pointing to the crotch, and waistline of pants may not reach natural waistline (arrow).

Adjustment. Lengthen the front and back pattern pieces an equal amount above hipline (page 52).

Short Legs

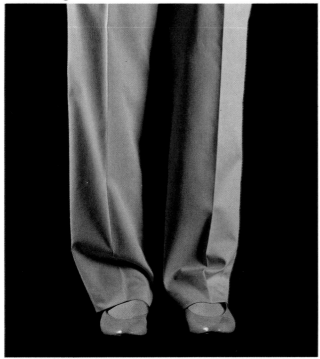

Problem. Legs are shorter than standard, causing pants legs that are too long.

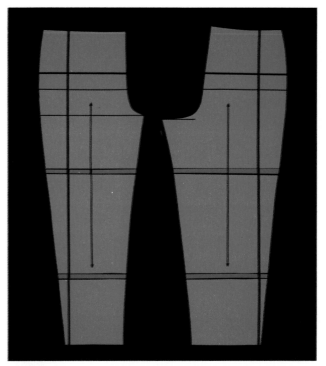

Adjustment. Shorten the front and back pattern pieces an equal amount above and below knee (page 53).

Long Legs

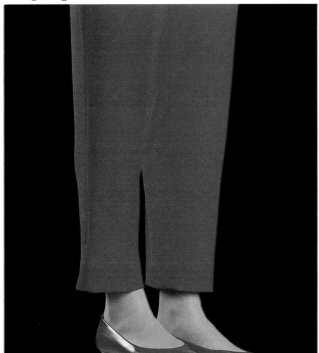

Problem. Legs are longer than standard, causing pants legs that are too short.

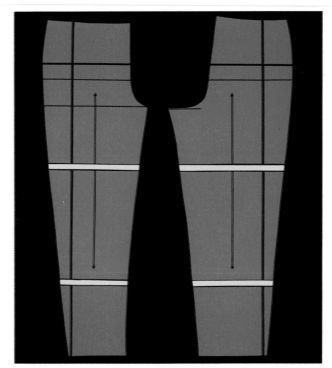

Adjustment. Lengthen the front and back pattern pieces an equal amount above and below knee (page 53).

Small Waist

Problem. Waist is smaller than standard, causing excess fabric at waistline. Waistband is too loose.

Adjustment. Lap upper sections an equal amount on front and back pattern pieces (page 54).

Large Waist

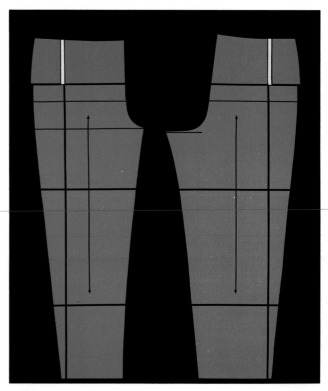

Problem. Waist is larger than standard, causing waistband that is too tight or does not close properly.

Adjustment. Spread upper sections an equal amount on front and back pattern pieces (page 54).

Small Hips

Problem. Hips are smaller than standard, causing vertical wrinkles to form in hip area and pants to bag at side seams.

Adjustment. Lap lower sections an equal amount on front and back pattern pieces (page 55).

Large Hips

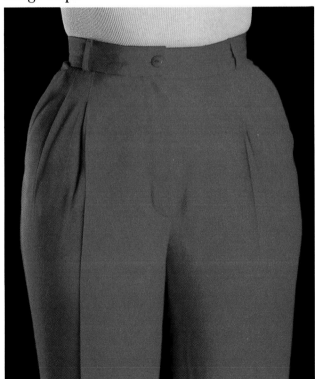

Problem. Hips are larger than standard, causing wrinkles to form across hip area and pocket openings and pleats to pull open.

Adjustment. Spread lower sections an equal amount on front and back pattern pieces (page 55).

Protruding Seat

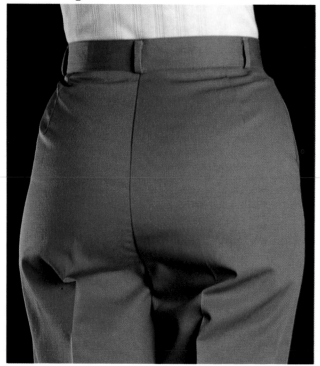

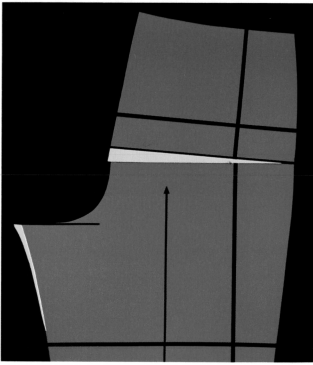

Problem. Seat protrudes more than standard, causing pants to dip in back at waistline and pull across seat. Wrinkles may form, pointing to fullness.

Adjustment. Spread back pattern piece to make wedge at hipline (pages 57 and 58). You may need to lengthen back crotch point (page 59).

Flat Seat

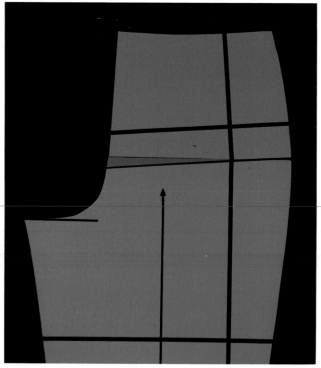

Problem. Seat is flatter than standard, causing pants to sag. Pants are baggy under seat and vertical wrinkles may form in back at waistline.

Adjustment. Lap back pattern piece to make wedge at hipline (pages 57 and 58). You may need to shorten back crotch point (page 59).

Prominent Abdomen

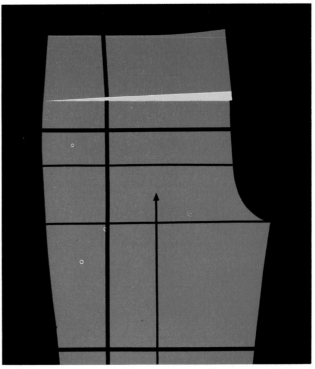

Problem. Abdomen is larger than standard, causing pants to dip in front at waistline and pull across abdomen. Wrinkles may form, pointing to fullness. Side seam may pull forward, and pleats are distorted.

Adjustment. Spread front pattern piece to make wedge at fullest part of abdomen (pages 57 and 58).

Protruding Front Thighs

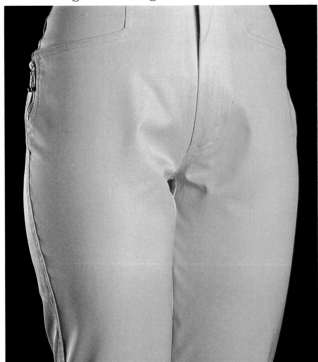

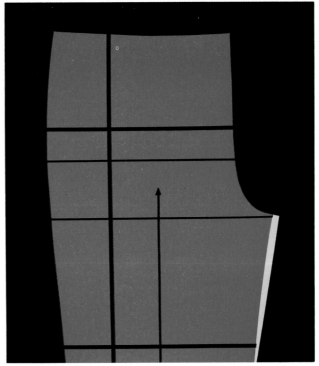

Problem. Thighs protrude in front more than standard, causing pants to pull across front crotch area. Horizontal wrinkles may form in crotch area. Pleats may not hang straight.

Adjustment. Lengthen front crotch point (page 59).

Knock-knees

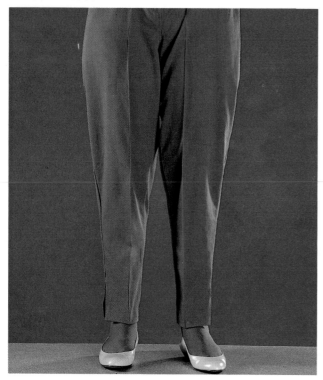

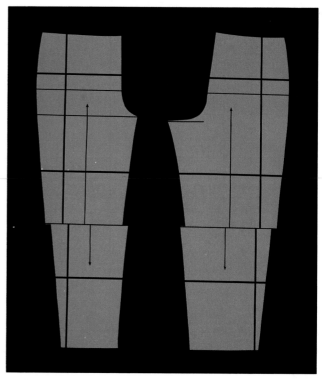

Problem. Legs bend toward each other at the knees. Pants rub against knee at inseam, causing diagonal lines to form; the problem may be more noticeable in the back.

Adjustment. Move lower sections below knee line toward inseam an equal amount on front and back pattern pieces (pages 54 and 55).

Bowlegs

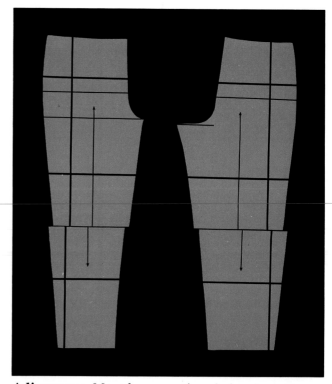

Problem. Legs bow out from the knees down. Pants rub against leg at or below the knee at side seam, causing diagonal lines to form.

Adjustment. Move lower sections below knee line toward side seam an equal amount on front and back pattern pieces (pages 54 and 55).

Combining Adjustments

Most people require more than one adjustment. The following examples may help you understand how several adjustments are made on one pattern.

Full Thighs

Sometimes one pattern adjustment solves more than one fitting problem. For example, if you select your pattern according to your hip measurement and make any necessary adjustments for a protruding seat or protruding front thighs, the pattern is automatically large enough for full thighs.

In the combination of adjustments below, the pattern is adjusted for both a protruding seat and protruding front thighs; this makes the crotch length longer and provides extra width in the thigh area at the same time.

Hip Tilt

When adjustments for a protruding seat are made, the pattern is adjusted for backward hip tilt without a separate adjustment. If you have forward hip tilt, make adjustment for a flat seat, and for protruding front thighs or prominent abdomen, if necessary.

In the combination of adjustments on page 42, the pattern is adjusted for long crotch depth, small waist, large hips, and protruding seat. A separate adjustment is not necessary for backward hip tilt.

Protruding Seat and Protruding Front Thighs

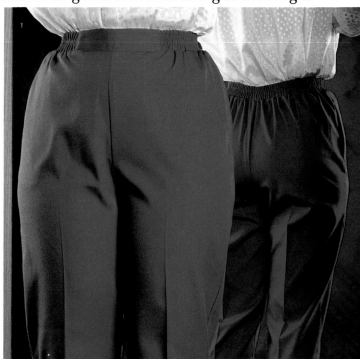

Problem. Protruding seat causes pants to dip in back at waistline and pull across seat; wrinkles may form, pointing to fullness. Protruding front thighs and full thighs cause pants to pull across thighs and front crotch area; horizontal wrinkles may form in crotch area and pleats may not hang straight.

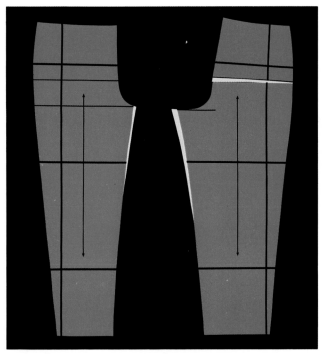

Adjustment. For protruding seat, spread back pattern piece to make a wedge at hipline (pages 57 and 58), and lengthen back crotch point (page 59). For protruding front thighs, lengthen front crotch point (page 59).

Long Crotch Depth, Small Waist, Large Hips, and Protruding Seat

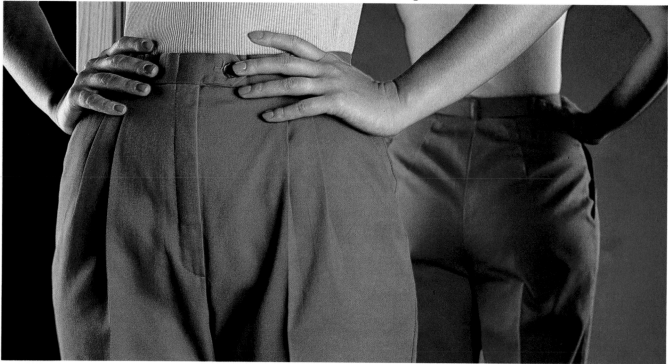

Problem. Long crotch depth causes pants to pull in crotch area and waistline of pants to fall below natural waistline. Small waist causes excess fabric at waistline, and waistband is too loose. Large hips cause wrinkles to form across hip area and pocket opening and pleats to pull open. Protruding seat causes pants to dip in back at waistline and pull across seat; wrinkles may form, pointing to fullness.

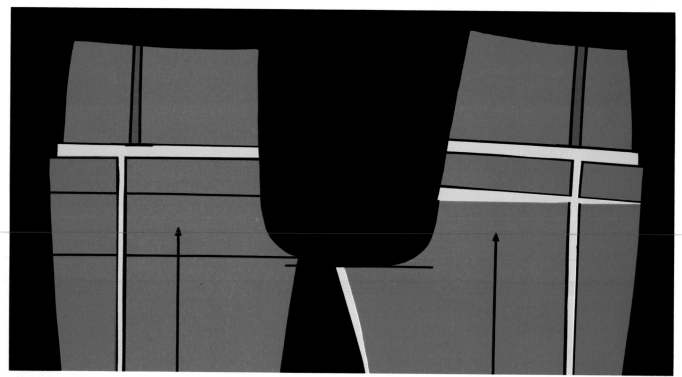

Adjustments. For long crotch depth, lengthen front and back pattern pieces an equal amount above hipline (page 52). For small waist, lap upper sections an equal amount on front and back pattern pieces (page 54). For large hips, spread lower sections an equal amount on front and back pattern pieces (page 55). For protruding seat, spread back pattern piece to make a wedge at hipline (pages 57 and 58); you may also need to lengthen back crotch point (page 59).

Pattern Adjustments

Four Steps to Pants That Fit

After you have taken your body measurements and have analyzed your figure, you are ready to transfer this information to the pattern and fabric. Fitting pants is a step-by-step process that includes both pattern and fitting adjustments.

In the pages that follow, the process of fitting pants has been broken down into four main steps. First, the pattern is prepared by marking adjustment lines on the pattern; pattern adjustments are made on these adjustment lines to avoid distorting the pattern shape

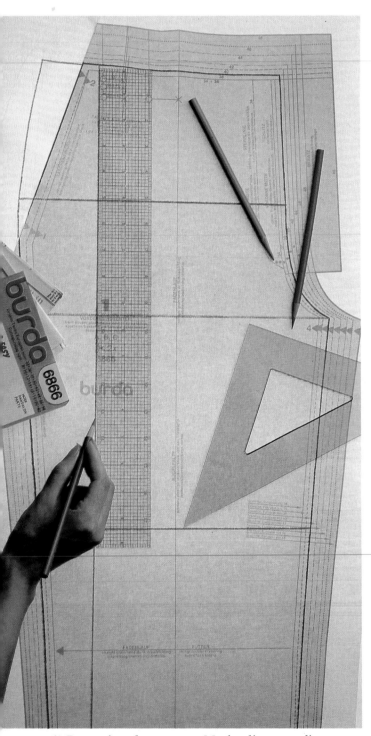

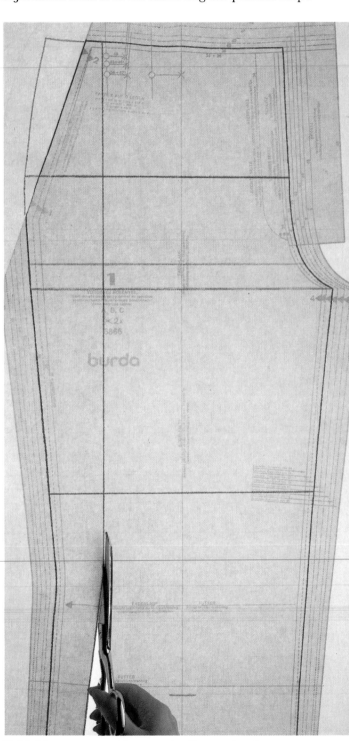

1) Preparing the pattern. Mark adjustment lines on the pattern tissue to prepare the pattern for making adjustments (pages 48 and 49).

2) Making pattern adjustments. Customize the pattern to your body by cutting along the adjustment lines and spreading or lapping the tissue (pages 50 to 59).

or design. Second, the pattern is adjusted to correspond to your body. The next step is trueing the pattern by redrawing the seamlines so they are smooth; wider seam allowances are added to allow room for fitting adjustments. Finally, the fit of the pants is perfected by making any minor fitting adjustments that may be necessary. These four steps have each been broken down into smaller steps, to simplify the fitting process and make it easier to understand.

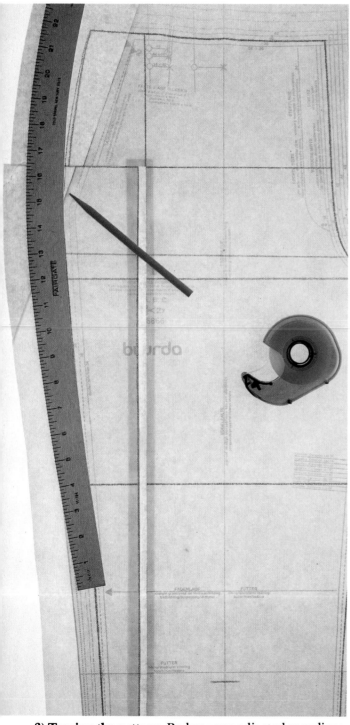

3) Trueing the pattern. Redraw any adjusted seamlines on the pattern. Add cutting lines, allowing wider seam allowances for fitting adjustments (pages 60 to 67).

4) Perfecting the fit. Cut and machine-baste the pants, and try them on. Then make any necessary minor adjustments (pages 70 to 85).

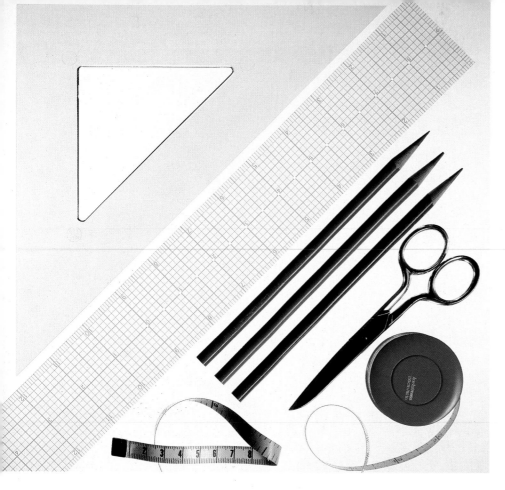

Preparing the Pattern

Pattern adjustments are made by lapping or spreading the pattern pieces. Four adjustment lines are drawn on the front pattern piece; then corresponding lines are drawn on the back piece. Length and width adjustments are made along these lines so the overall shape of the pattern is not distorted.

Leave about 2" (5 cm) excess tissue around pattern pieces. The excess tissue may be needed for adjustments or for trueing lines.

If pattern has a slant pocket, use the side pocket piece as a guide for extending the waistline and side seamline to prepare the pattern for adjustments.

How to Prepare the Pattern for Fitting Adjustments

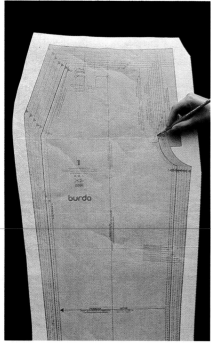

1) Cut around pants front and back pattern pieces, leaving about 2" (5 cm) of excess tissue. Press tissue flat. When using multisized pattern, draw along all seamlines for the selected size.

2) Draw crotch line on pants front, perpendicular to grainline, from front crotch point to side seamline.

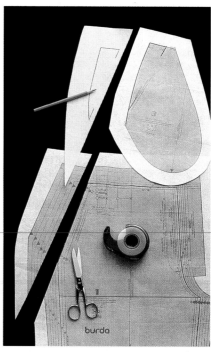

3) Trace, on separate tissue, portion of side pocket piece that extends from waistline to side seamline on pattern with slant pocket. Cut along pocket opening on pants front. Align traced piece to pocket opening; tape in place.

How to Draw Adjustment Lines

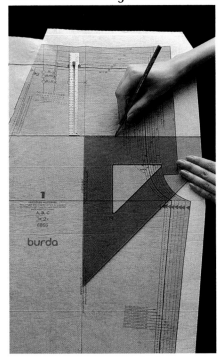

Line 1. Draw line, perpendicular to grainline, 5" (12.5 cm) down from the waistline.

Line 2. Fold hemline to crotch line to determine knee line; crease fold. Draw line halfway between crotch line and knee line, perpendicular to grainline.

Line 3. Draw line halfway between knee line and hemline, perpendicular to grainline.

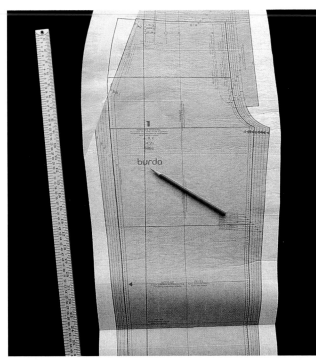

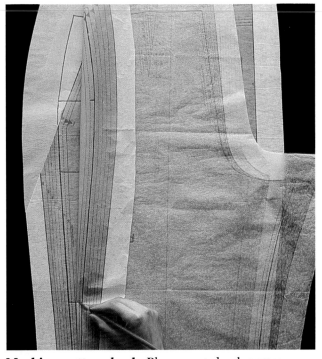

Line 4. Draw line, parallel to grainline, from waistline to hemline, about 3" (7.5 cm) in from side seamline in hip area; avoid extending line into pleat or dart space, if possible.

Marking pattern back. Place pants back pattern on top of pants front, matching side seamlines. Fold back the edge of pattern back, and mark Lines 1, 2, and 3 at side seamline. Mark Line 4 at waistline and hemline. Complete lines on pattern back by drawing them square to grainline.

Pattern Adjustments

After adjustment lines are drawn on the pattern, you are ready to make the pattern adjustments. It is important to follow the correct sequence, below, as you make the adjustments in this section.

Length adjustments are made first, followed by any width adjustments. Complete all the length and width adjustments on the front pattern piece; then adjust the back pattern piece by the same amount.

Sequence of Adjustments

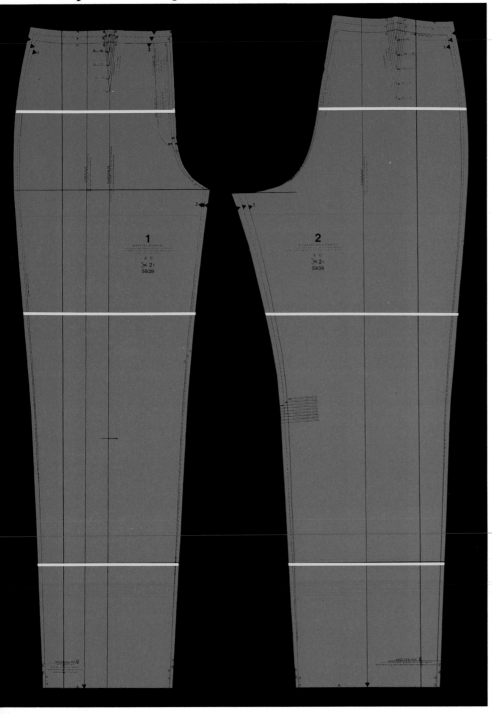

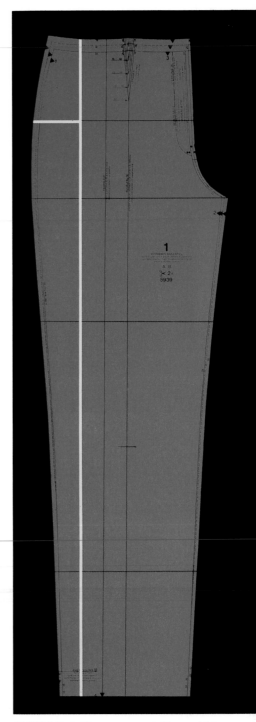

1) Length Adjustments. Adjust crotch depth (page 52) to lengthen or shorten pattern between waistline and crotch line. Then lengthen or shorten pants legs (page 53) above and below knee line.

2) Width Adjustments. Adjust width of waistline by moving upper side

All sections requiring length and width adjustments are moved parallel or perpendicular to the grainline and to other sections, to maintain the original grainline.

After completing the length and width adjustments, adjust the crotch length by adding wedges or by changing the crotch points.

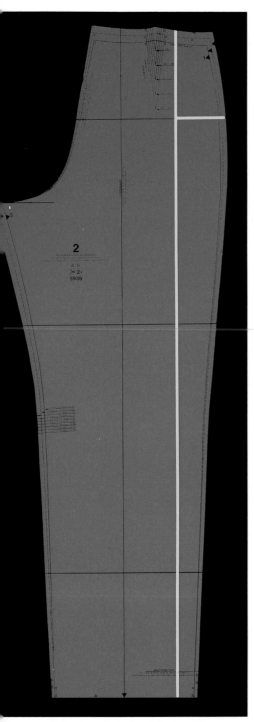

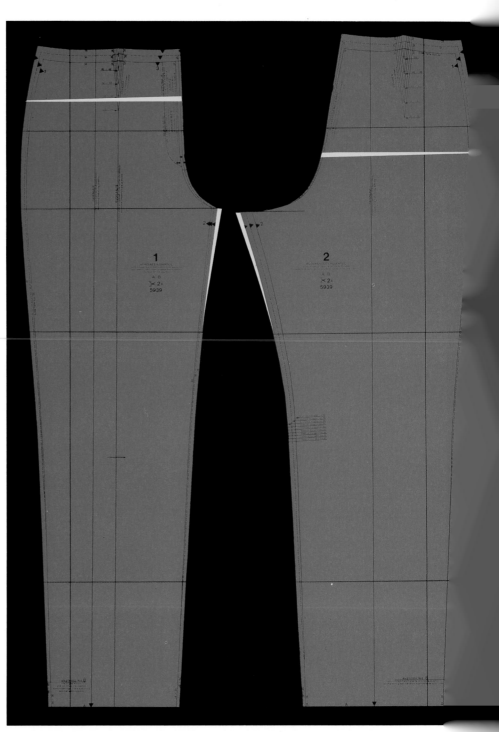

section (page 54). Adjust hipline by moving lower side section (page 55).

3) Crotch Length Adjustments. Crotch length can be adjusted by making wedges or by changing crotch points (pages 56 to 59). One or both types of adjustments may be needed.

Making Length Adjustments

How to Adjust the Crotch Depth

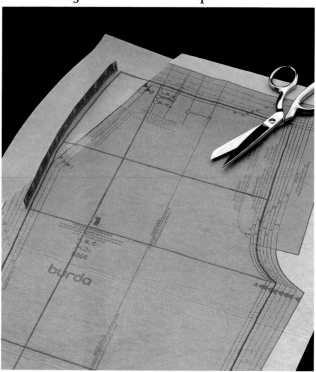

Compare your body measurements to the pattern measurements to determine any length adjustments needed and record this information on the Pants Adjustments Chart (pages 30 and 31). If the length of the pattern between the waistline and the crotch line needs to be adjusted, make this adjustment first, by adjusting the crotch depth. Then adjust the length of the pants legs, if necessary.

Spread or lap the pattern sections along the adjustment line, keeping the adjustment lines parallel.

Adjusting the Crotch Depth

Compare your crotch depth measurement plus ease to the front pattern piece along the side seamline. After adjusting the crotch depth on the front pattern piece, adjust the back pattern piece the same amount.

1) Measure along side seamline of pattern front from waistline to crotch line. Compare pattern measurement to your crotch depth measurement plus ease. Difference is adjustment needed.

2a) Lengthen crotch depth by spreading pattern along Line 1. Adjust front and back an equal amount.

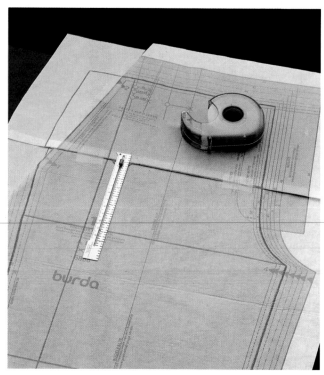

2b) Shorten crotch depth by lapping pattern along Line 1. Adjust front and back an equal amount.

Adjusting the Length of the Pants Legs

Compare your measurement from the waist to just below the ankle bone to the pattern piece from the waistline to the hemline.

The length of the pants legs is usually adjusted equally on Lines 2 and 3. Occasionally a pants pattern may have a design detail that requires careful placement on the leg, as in pants with seaming at the knee, or jodhpurs. Then the amount of adjustment may be divided unequally on Line 2 and Line 3, so the design detail will be in the right place.

The standard hemline of full-length pants is just below the ankle bone. However, pants lengths vary, depending on the style of the pants and your personal preference.

How to Adjust the Length of the Pants Legs

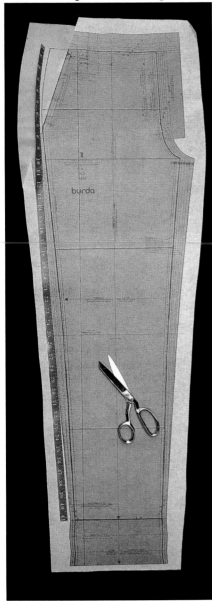
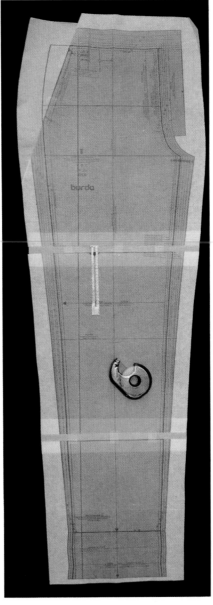

1) Measure pattern along side seamline from waistline to hemline. Compare pattern measurement to your measurement. Difference is adjustment needed.

2a) Lengthen pants legs by spreading pattern equally on Line 2 and Line 3. Adjust front and back an equal amount.

2b) Shorten pants legs by lapping pattern equally on Line 2 and Line 3. Adjust front and back an equal amount.

Making Width Adjustments

Compare your body measurements to the pattern measurements to determine any width adjustments needed, and record this information on the Pants Adjustment Chart (pages 30 and 31). Adjust the width of the pattern by making any waistline or hipline adjustments required. Spread or lap the pattern sections along the adjustment line, keeping the adjustment lines parallel.

Adjusting the Waistline

The standard amount of ease allowed at the waistline is 1" (2.5 cm); ½" (1.3 cm) of fabric is eased to the waistband, and the finished waistband is ½" (1.3 cm) larger than your waist measurement. If you prefer a looser fit, allow 1½" (3.8 cm) of ease, so the waistband will be 1" (2.5 cm) larger than your waist measurement.

If you have a prominent abdomen or full, high hips, adjust the waistline of the pattern so it is 2" (5 cm) larger than your waist measurement, to provide the ease needed in the area below the waistline. During the fitting, the seams, darts, and pleats are then adjusted to perfect the fit at the waist, abdomen, and high hips.

If an adjustment of ½" (1.3 cm) or less is needed, the waistline may be adjusted by changing the depth of the darts, pleats, or side seams, instead of by adjusting the pattern.

Adjusting the Hipline

The amount of ease the pattern allows at the hipline varies with each pattern company and style of pants.

It may be necessary to make a pattern adjustment at the hipline, even if you have selected the pattern according to the hip measurement. Some patterns have the standard hipline marked on the pattern tissue, but you should draw your own hipline on the pattern after the crotch depth adjustment has been made, and measure the amount of ease at your hipline.

The standard amount of fitting ease allowed at the hipline in dart-fitted pants is 2" (5 cm). For pleated pants, allow a minimum of 1" (2.5 cm) of fitting ease; large sizes may need more. To determine the amount of fitting ease allowed in a pleated pants pattern, fold out the pleats before measuring the pattern, to eliminate the design ease. The fold for a deep pleat will be longer than that for a shallow pleat, which may be only as long as a dart.

After adjusting the pattern, mark a new center grainline on the pattern and change the pleat placement lines so the foldline of the major pleat lines up with the new center grainline (page 89).

Adjusting for Bowlegs or Knock-knees

A pattern adjustment of ½" to 1½" (1.3 to 3.8 cm) can be made for bowlegs or knock-knees. After adjusting the pattern, mark a new center grainline and change the pleat placement so the foldline of the major pleat lines up with the new center grainline (page 89).

How to Adjust the Waistline

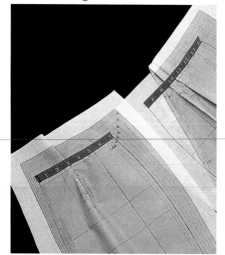  

1) Fold out darts or pleats. Measure waistline of pattern front and back. Double this measurement and compare it to your waist measurement plus ease. Divide any difference by 4; this is the amount to adjust.

2a) Increase waistline by spreading Line 4 above Line 1 one-fourth total amount needed. Adjust front and back an equal amount.

2b) Decrease waistline by lapping Line 4 above Line 1 one-fourth total amount needed. Adjust front and back an equal amount.

How to Adjust the Hipline

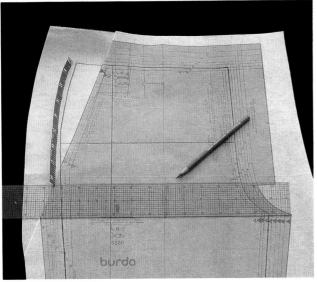

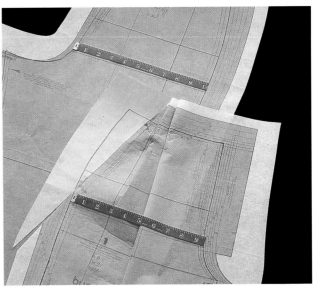

1) Measure along side seamline of pattern front, from waistline to hip depth position recorded on Pants Adjustment Chart (pages 30 and 31). Draw hipline perpendicular to grainline. Repeat on pattern back.

2) Fold out darts or pleats. Measure hipline of pattern front and back. Double this measurement and compare it to your hip measurement plus ease. Divide any difference by 4; this is the amount to adjust.

How to Adjust for Bowlegs or Knock-knees

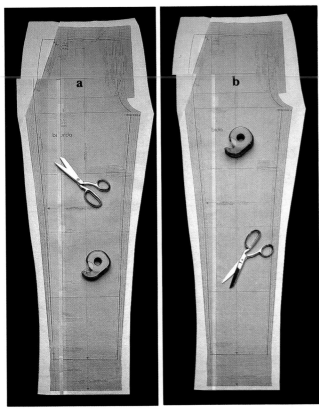

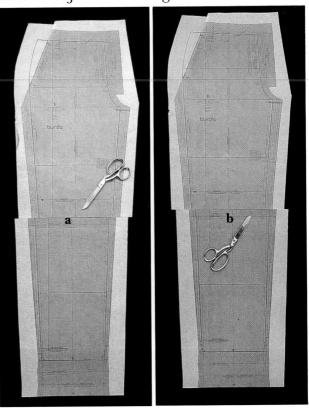

3) Increase hipline **(a)** by spreading Line 4 below Line 1 one-fourth total amount needed, or decrease hipline **(b)** by lapping Line 4 below Line 1 one-fourth total amount needed. Adjust front and back an equal amount. Mark new center grainline (page 89).

Measure along side seamline, from waistline to knee position recorded on Pants Adjustment Chart (pages 30 and 31). Draw knee line perpendicular to grainline. Move lower section ½" to 1½" (1.3 to 3.8 cm) toward side seam for bowlegs **(a),** or toward inseam for knock-knees **(b)**. Adjust front and back an equal amount. Mark new center grainline (page 89).

Making Crotch Length Adjustments

Compare your body crotch length plus ease to the pattern crotch length, to determine any adjustments you may need. Record this information on the Pants Adjustment Chart (pages 30 and 31). The crotch length and the angle of the crotch seam are adjusted, based on the fitting problems you have had in the past and the visual analysis of your body.

Three pattern adjustments affect the crotch length: changing the crotch depth, making wedges, and changing the crotch points. By using one or more of these adjustments, you can make any crotch length changes exactly where they are needed.

The way your pants fit can indicate the adjustments needed. For example, if your pants usually dip at the back waistline, add to the crotch length by spreading a wedge for a protruding seat; use the amount that the pants dip at the waistline as a guide to the size of the wedge. Or if your pants usually ride up at the back waistline and are baggy under the seat, reduce the back crotch length by lapping a wedge for a flat seat.

Read through all the information on how to adjust the crotch length and the angle of the crotch seam before making any pattern changes. If any wedge adjustments are needed, make them first. Then calculate the amount of change you still need, and adjust the crotch points.

If, after making wedge and crotch point adjustments, the adjusted crotch length is close to the measurement needed, the crotch length can still be adjusted slightly by reshaping the crotch curve (page 79). This final adjustment should be made at the fitting, when you can see how the pants look on you.

The amount of ease for crotch length on the Pants Adjustment Chart is a guideline; this amount is appropriate for a basic or classic pattern. Personal preferences vary, and different styles of pants require different amounts of ease. For example, blue jeans may be fitted very close to the body, while pants with deep pleats may require a greater amount of ease.

Determining the Crotch Length Adjustments

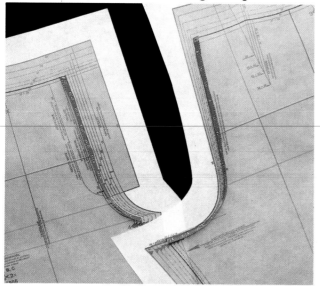

1) Measure front and back crotch seamlines of pattern to determine pattern crotch length. Compare pattern measurement to body measurement plus ease. The difference is the adjustment needed.

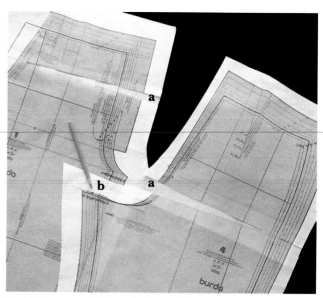

2) Adjust crotch length by making wedges (**a**), as on pages 57 and 58, or by changing the crotch points (**b**), as on page 59. Depending on your body analysis, you may need one or more types of adjustment.

Wedge Adjustments

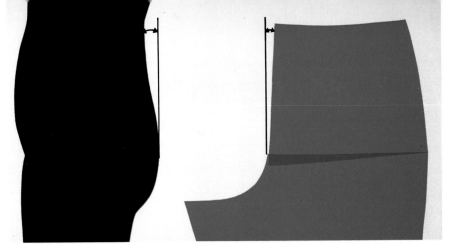

Spread or lap the pants pattern to make a wedge adjustment. By making a wedge, you can adjust the crotch length and the angle of the back crotch seam for a protruding seat or a flat seat. Spread the pattern to make a wedge for a prominent abdomen. No adjustment is needed for a flat abdomen; wedges are never lapped on the front pattern piece. Wedge adjustments are often made in combination with changes in the crotch points to achieve the correct crotch length measurement and the angle of the crotch seam.

The size of the wedge depends on how much your body varies from the standard. If there is a slight protrusion of the seat or abdomen, spread the pattern a small amount; if there is a greater protrusion, make the wedge larger. If your seat is flat, lap the wedge at the back hipline. Lapping or spreading the pattern a small amount can make a significant change in the way the pants fit.

It is necessary to lap the back wedge and spread the front wedge if you have a flat seat and a prominent abdomen.

Flat seat. Lap the back pattern piece to make a wedge adjustment. This shortens the crotch length and reduces the angle to the waistline on the pattern, so it corresponds to the angle of the body.

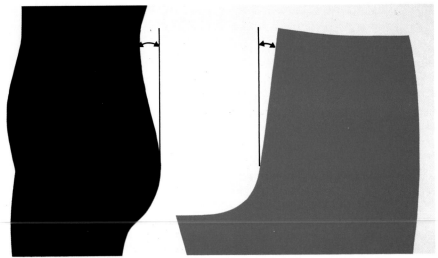

Standard seat corresponds to pattern piece without making a wedge adjustment. The crotch length does not need to be adjusted in the seat area, and the angle of the pattern corresponds to the angle of the body.

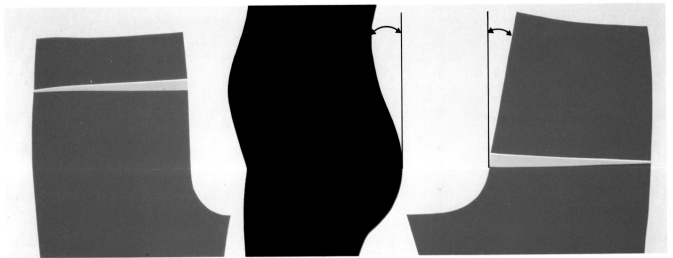

Protruding seat and prominent abdomen. Spread the back pattern piece to make a wedge adjustment for a protruding seat. This lengthens the crotch length and increases the angle to the waistline on the pattern, so it corresponds to the angle of the body. Spread the front pattern piece to make a wedge adjustment for a prominent abdomen. This lengthens the crotch length and allows more room for the abdomen. Redraw front crotch seamline so angle of seam is not changed, page 58, step 3.

How to Make a Wedge Adjustment for a Protruding or Flat Seat

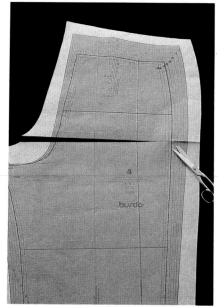

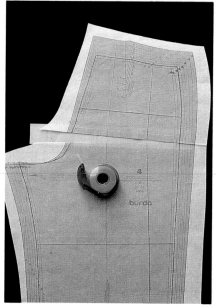

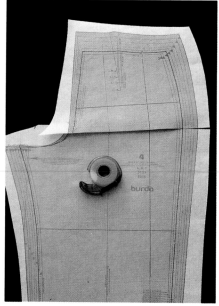

1) Draw hipline on pattern back, page 55, step 1. Slash pattern on hipline from crotch seamline to, but not through, side seamline. Cut from edge of tissue at hipline to side seamline, taking care not to cut pattern apart.

2a) Protruding seat. Spread pattern on slashed line, to a maximum of 1½" (3.8 cm), pivoting at side seamline. If more crotch length is needed, lengthen back crotch point, opposite.

2b) Flat seat. Lap pattern on slashed line, pivoting at side seamline. For maximum adjustment, lap pattern until center back seamline is parallel to grainline. Additional crotch length may be removed at back crotch point, opposite.

How to Make a Wedge Adjustment for a Prominent Abdomen

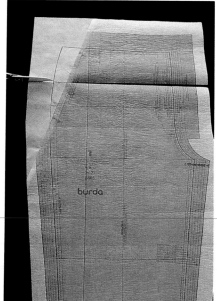

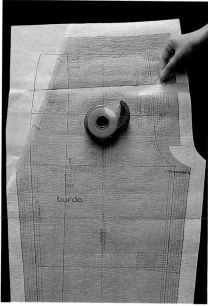

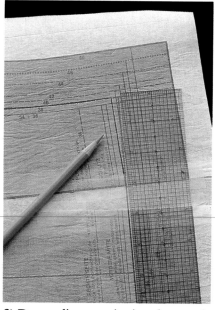

1) Draw a line on pattern front at fullest part of abdomen, about 3" (7.5 cm) from waistline, parallel to Line 1. Slash pattern on line from center front to, but not through, side seamline. Cut from edge of tissue at adjustment line to side seamline, taking care not to cut pattern apart.

2) Spread pattern on slashed line, to a maximum of 1½" (3.8 cm), pivoting at side seamline. If more crotch length is needed, lengthen back crotch point, opposite.

3) Draw a line, continuing the crotch seamline from below the wedge to the waistline. This adjustment also increases waistline slightly; the added width may be eased to waistband or added to front darts or pleats.

Adjusting the Crotch Points

The crotch points of the pattern are adjusted to accommodate full thighs or protruding front thighs, or to achieve the correct crotch length when making other adjustments. For example, you may adjust the back crotch point in addition to making a wedge adjustment for a prominent abdomen or for a protruding or flat seat.

To adjust a pattern for protruding front thighs, the front crotch point can be lengthened to a maximum of ½" (1.3 cm); for full thigh adjustments, see page 41. All other crotch point adjustments are made on the back crotch point. The front and back pattern pieces are adjusted individually; you may need to shorten one and lengthen the other.

The type of pattern you select will make a difference in the amount of change needed at the crotch points, right. If additional crotch length is needed after making wedge adjustments and adjusting the crotch points, remeasure to check the accuracy of the crotch depth and crotch length measurements. It may be necessary to increase the crotch depth slightly or to reshape the crotch curve (page 79).

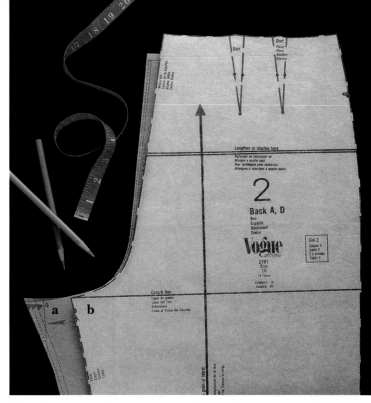

Crotch points of patterns vary, depending on type of pattern selected. Patterns with longer back crotch points **(a)** may be lengthened up to 2" (5 cm). Patterns with shorter back crotch points **(b)** may be lengthened at the crotch point up to 3¼" (8.1 cm).

How to Change the Placement of Crotch Points

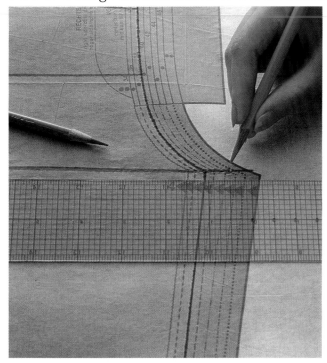

Front crotch point. Lengthen crotch line on pattern front through crotch point. Lengthen front crotch point by measuring from original crotch point, along crotch line, and marking adjustment needed, to a maximum of ½" (1.3 cm). If more crotch length is needed, lengthen the back crotch point.

Back crotch point. Draw a line through back crotch point parallel to Line 1; extend line about 4" (10 cm) on either side of inseam. Lengthen or shorten back crotch point by measuring from original crotch point, along crotch line, and marking adjustment needed.

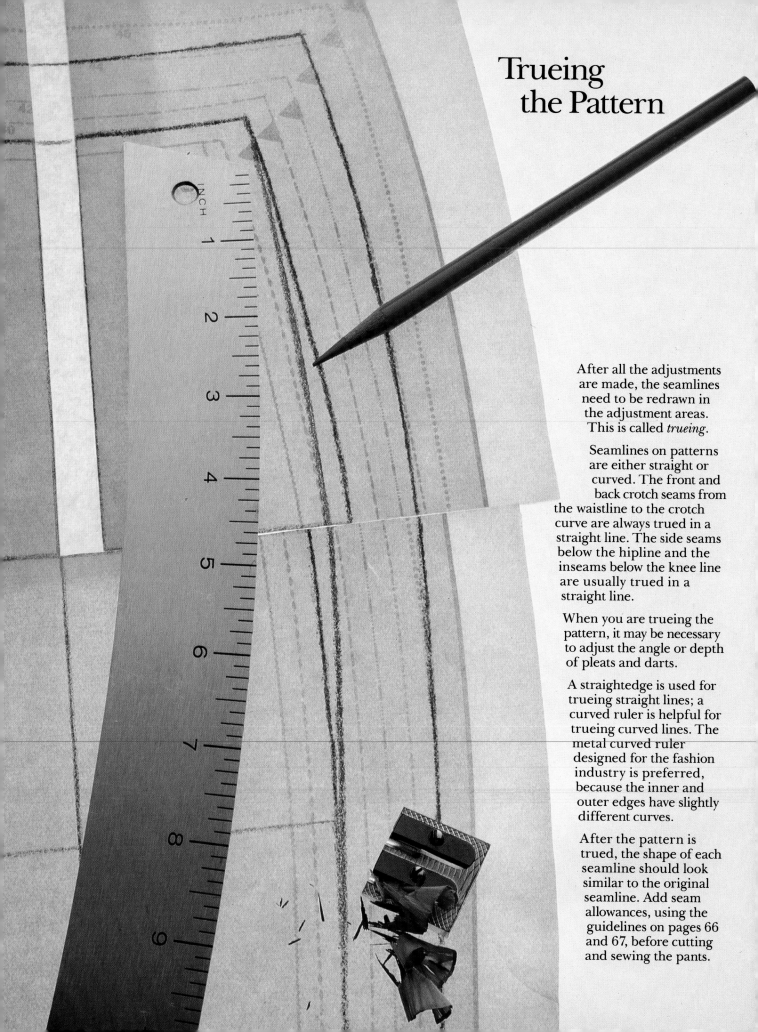

Trueing the Pattern

After all the adjustments are made, the seamlines need to be redrawn in the adjustment areas. This is called *trueing*.

Seamlines on patterns are either straight or curved. The front and back crotch seams from the waistline to the crotch curve are always trued in a straight line. The side seams below the hipline and the inseams below the knee line are usually trued in a straight line.

When you are trueing the pattern, it may be necessary to adjust the angle or depth of pleats and darts.

A straightedge is used for trueing straight lines; a curved ruler is helpful for trueing curved lines. The metal curved ruler designed for the fashion industry is preferred, because the inner and outer edges have slightly different curves.

After the pattern is trued, the shape of each seamline should look similar to the original seamline. Add seam allowances, using the guidelines on pages 66 and 67, before cutting and sewing the pants.

How to True the Waistline (waistline or hipline adjustment)

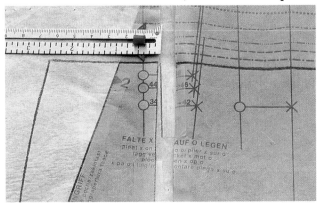

1) Adjust pleats or darts to original depth, if waistline adjustment has changed them.

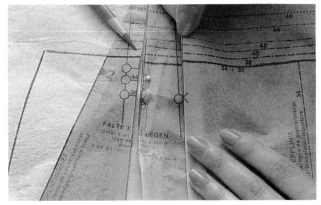

2) Fold darts or pleats in the direction they are to be pressed during construction. Draw slightly curved line to true waistline.

How to True the Waistline (prominent abdomen adjustment)

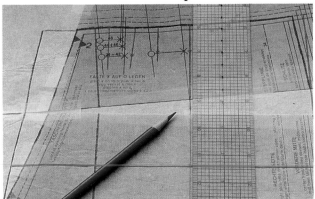

1) Reposition outside fold of major pleat above wedge adjustment line so outside fold is on center grainline. Adjust depth and angle of pleats or darts. Fold pleats or darts in place.

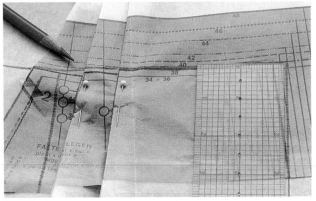

2) Eliminate peak at center front by drawing a line about 1" (2.5 cm) long at right angle to previously adjusted front crotch seamline, page 58, step 3. Draw slightly curved line, tapering to side seamline and center front, to true waistline.

How to True the Side Seamlines

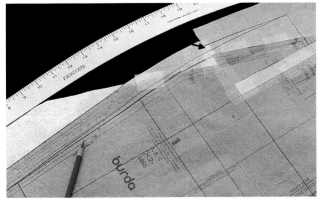

Waistline or crotch depth adjustment. Draw slightly curved line to true side seamline from waistline through center of jog (arrow); extend line to or beyond hipline, as far as necessary for a smooth line. True side seamline below hipline, following original pattern shape. Repeat exactly for pattern back.

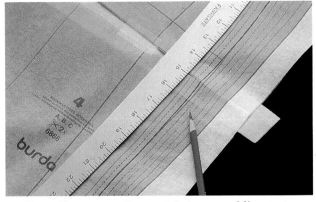

Wedge adjustment. Draw slightly curved line to true side seamline, eliminating indentation formed when wedge was made.

How to True the Inseam

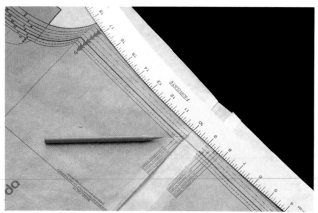

Front leg length adjustment. Draw slightly curved line to true inseam from crotch point through center of jog at Line 2 to knee area. True inseam below knee area following original pattern shape.

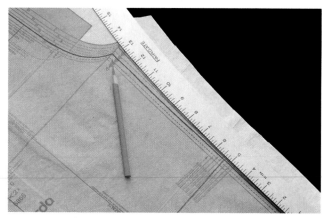

Front crotch point adjustment. Draw slightly curved line to true inseam from new crotch point to knee area.

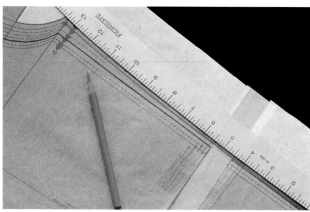

Front leg length and crotch point adjustment. Draw slightly curved line to true inseam from new crotch point to knee area; do not draw new seamline through center of jog at Line 2. True inseam below knee area following original pattern shape.

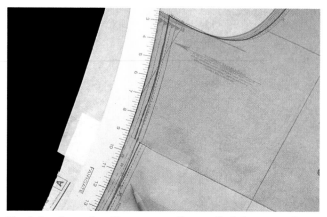

Back leg length adjustment. Draw slightly curved line to true inseam from crotch point through center of jog at Line 2; extend to a point midway between Line 2 and knee line. True inseam below knee area following original pattern shape.

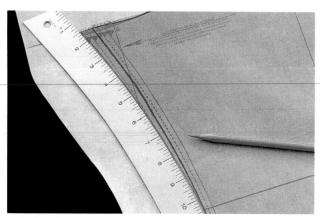

Minor back crotch point adjustment. Draw slightly curved line to true inseam from crotch point; taper to original inseam near Line 2. Blend new inseam slightly lower if leg length adjustment was also made, and true inseam below knee area following original pattern shape.

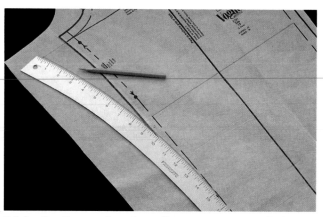

Major back crotch point adjustment. Draw slightly curved line to true inseam from crotch point; taper to original inseam slightly above knee area.

How to True the Front Crotch Seamline

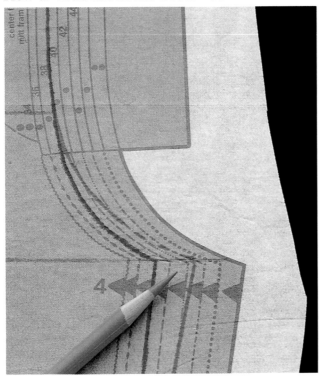

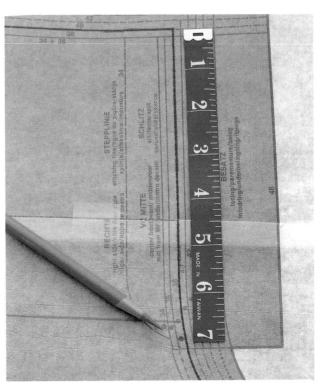

1) True crotch seamline from where it begins to curve, extending to new crotch point.

2) Adjust fly facing for 7" to 9" (18 to 23 cm) zipper opening, if crotch depth was lengthened or shortened.

How to True the Back Crotch Seamline

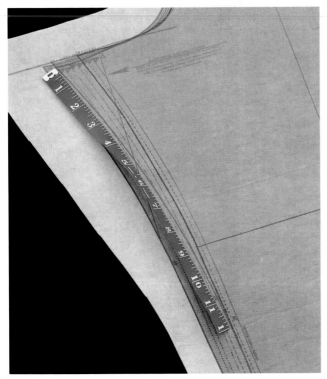

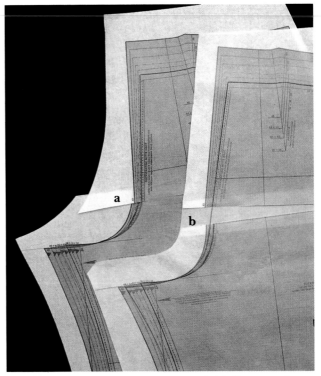

1) Measure length of original inseam from crotch line to end of trueing if crotch point was adjusted; measure new inseam in same area. Difference between measurements is amount to lower crotch point. True crotch curve to new crotch point.

2) True smooth line from waistline to hipline, curving to crotch point. If wedge adjustment was made, curve varies, depending on whether wedge was overlapped **(a)** or expanded **(b)**.

How to True a Side-seam Pocket

1) Measure the length of original pocket opening on pattern front.

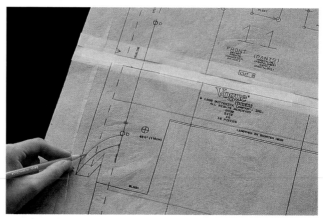

2) Mark lower end of pocket opening the length of original opening; redraw lower edge of pocket extension. True seamline of extension in straight line. If wedge adjustment was made, true waistline, as for pocket with stay, steps 2 and 3, opposite.

How to True a Slant Pocket without a Pocket Stay

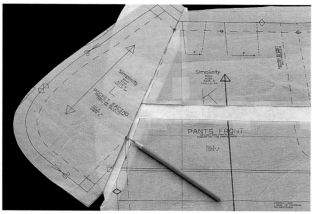

1) Align pocket facing to waistline and match lower end of pocket opening with trued side seamline. Mark lower end of pocket opening on pattern front.

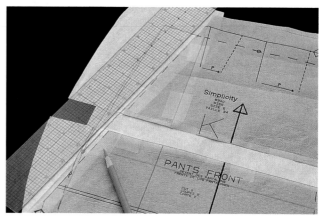

2) Draw a new pocket opening seamline, using a straightedge.

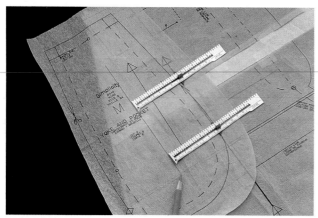

3) Fold under pattern front along pocket opening seamline. Lay side pocket piece over pattern front, matching pocket opening markings. Draw new grainline on side pocket piece parallel to grainline on pattern front.

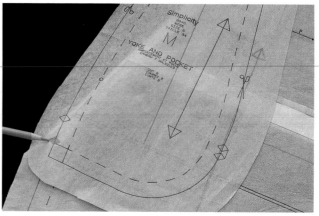

4) Trace pattern markings onto side pocket piece. Repeat steps 3 and 4 for pocket facing. If wedge adjustment was made, true waistline, if necessary, as for pocket with stay, steps 2 and 3, opposite.

How to True a Slant Pocket with a Pocket Stay

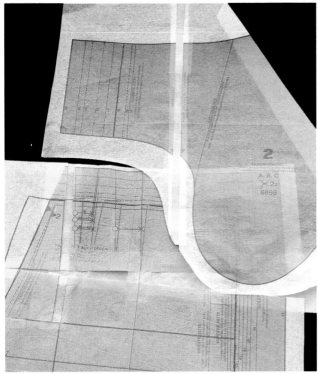

1) Follow steps 1 to 4 for slant pocket, opposite. If width adjustment was made on pattern front, cut stay portion of pocket facing parallel to grainline. Adjust width of pocket facing same amount as pattern front.

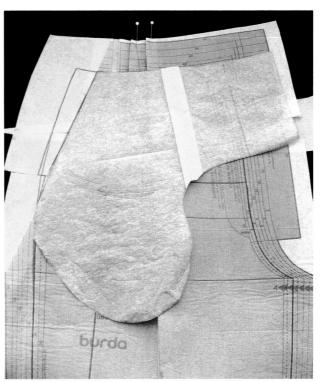

2) Fold out pleats or darts, if width or wedge adjustment was made on pattern front. Lay pocket facing over pattern front; align it to trued seamlines at pocket opening and side seamline. (Pattern has been trimmed at seamlines to show detail.)

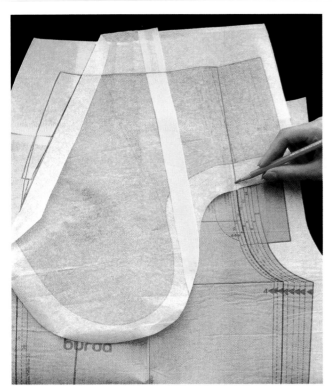

3) Trace new seamline at waistline and new center front line, if width or wedge adjustment was made on pattern front.

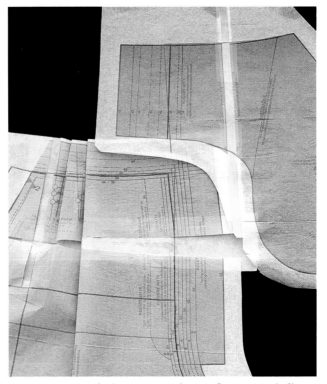

4) Turn pocket facing over, and transfer new waistline and center front line to right side of pattern. True lower edge of pocket facing.

How to Add Seam and Hem Allowances on Pants

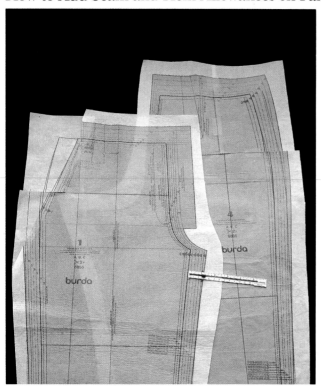

1) Add 1" (2.5 cm) seam allowances at side seamlines and inseams.

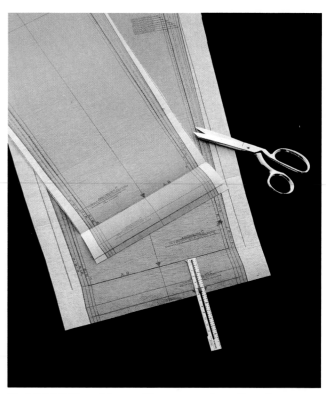

2) Add 2" (5 cm) hem allowance at hemline for pants without cuffs. Fold pattern at hemline; trim pattern on cutting lines.

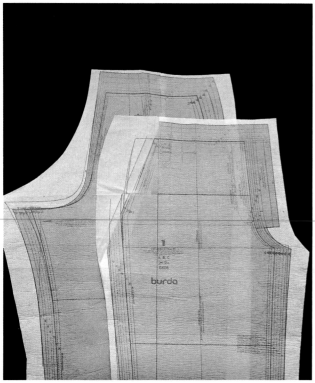

3) Add 1½" (3.8 cm) at center front for fly facing. Add ⅝" (1.5 cm) seam allowances at front and back crotch seams and at pocket opening of slant pocket.

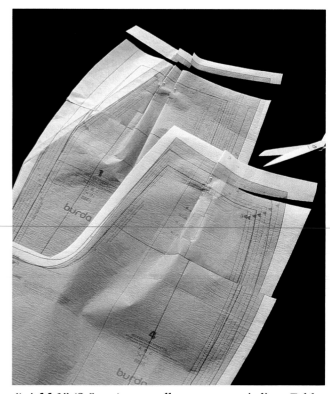

4) Add 1" (2.5 cm) seam allowance at waistline. Fold darts and pleats in direction they are to be pressed, matching markings; trim pattern on cutting line to true darts and pleats.

How to Add Seam Allowances on Pockets

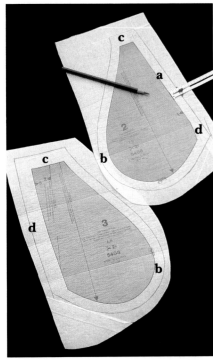
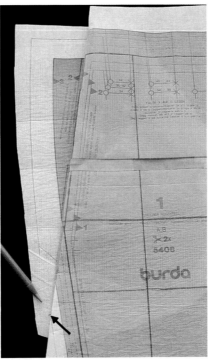
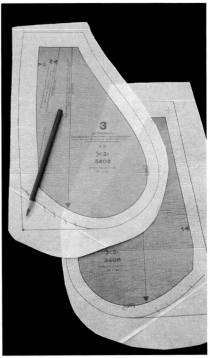

Slant pocket. 1) Add ⅝" (1.5 cm) seam allowance to pocket opening **(a)** on pocket facing and to curved edges **(b)** of both pocket pieces. Add 1" (2.5 cm) seam allowance at waistline **(c)** and side seamline **(d)** of both pieces.

2) Fold under pattern front at seamline of pocket opening; align opening to placement line on side pocket piece. Mark a dot at side cutting line (arrow). Extend 1" (2.5 cm) seam allowance on pocket piece to dot, if necessary.

3) Draw horizontal line from dot to curved cutting line on side pocket piece. Repeat for pocket facing.

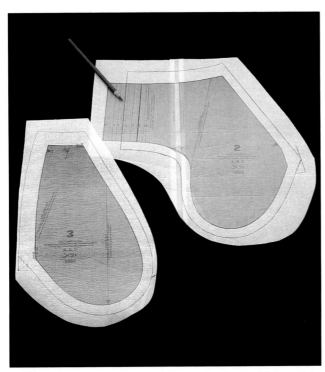

Pocket with stay. Follow steps 1 to 3, above. Then add 1" (2.5 cm) seam allowance beyond center front.

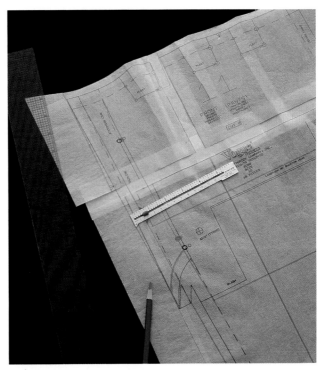

Side-seam pocket. Add ⅝" (1.5 cm) seam allowance to lower end of pocket opening and to pocket extension.

Perfecting the Fit

Getting Ready for the Fitting

After the pattern adjustments are made, you are ready to sew the pants. You can sew them from the final garment fabric instead of making trial or test pants. Prepare the fabric by preshrinking it before sewing, using the care method recommended by the manufacturer. This prevents the pants from shrinking and the seams from puckering. To preshrink fabric that requires dry cleaning, steam it evenly with a steam iron and allow it to dry flat.

Cutting & Marking

Cut out the pants with 1" (2.5 cm) seam allowances at the waistline, side seamlines, and inseams, to allow for any minor adjustments you may need. Lay out the front and back pattern pieces, following the guidelines on the instruction sheet. If a pocket piece will be visible when the pants are worn, such as the side pocket piece for a slant pocket, cut it from pants fabric. Cut pocket facings from lining fabric to reduce bulk.

Instead of adjusting the waistband pattern piece to fit you, mark the width and length for the waistband on the fabric. The standard finished width of a waistband is 1¼" (3.2 cm), but some styles of pants may have wider waistbands. If you have high, full hips,

a 1" (2.5 cm) or narrower waistband may be more comfortable. The waistband piece is cut longer than necessary, but it is trimmed to the correct length during the waistband construction (page 107).

Use tailor's tacks for marking the pants. Do not use a marking pen or chalk to transfer pattern markings; marks from a marking pen cannot be pressed over, and chalk may rub off during the fittings. Keep the tailor's tacks in place, even after machine-basting the pants, to use as a reference for transferring any fitting adjustments to the pattern.

Machine-basting the Pants

For pants with creases, it is easier to position the crease accurately if the creases are lightly pressed on the center grainline before the pants are machine-basted. If you do not plan to crease the pants, mark the center grainline with hand basting.

The pants are then machine-basted for the fitting, using six to eight stitches per inch (2.5 cm), so minor adjustments at the seamlines can be made easily. Lightly press the seams flat to make it easier to check the fit.

How to Cut Out the Pants

1) Cut waistband along selvage, with length of waistband 4½" (11.5 cm) longer than waist measurement and width twice the desired finished width plus ⅞" (2.2 cm).

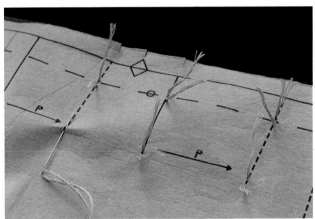

2) Follow pattern guide sheet to lay out remainder of pants. Cut seam allowances as marked (pages 66 and 67). Cut side pocket piece for slant pocket from pants fabric. Cut pocket facings from lining fabric.

How to Mark the Pants

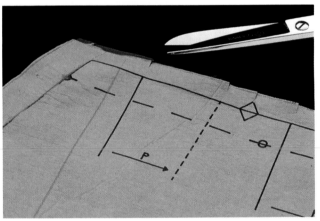

1) Make ¼" (6 mm) clip into seam allowance to mark center front, ends of darts and pleats, and notches.

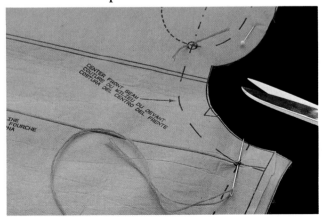

2) Mark all other pattern markings with speed tailor's tacks, below, including darts, tucks, pocket opening and bottom of zipper opening; also mark front and back crotch points.

How to Make Speed Tailor's Tacks

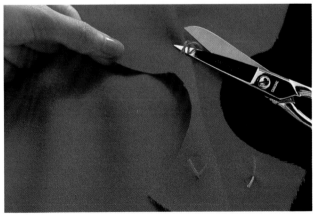

1) Use long length of 6-strand embroidery floss or darning cotton. Take stitch through pattern marking, leaving 1" (2.5 cm) tail at beginning and end.

2) Lift pattern from fabric carefully. Separate fabric layers no more than ½" (1.3 cm). Clip threads, leaving thread tufts on each layer of fabric.

How to Assemble Pants for Fitting

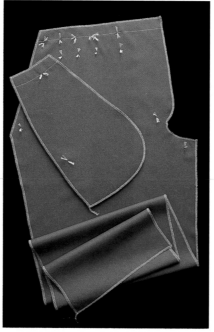

1) Mark waistline with row of basting stitches.

2) Finish all raw edges of fabric that will ravel, using overlock or zigzag stitch.

3) Fold dart, right sides together, matching markings. Using a straightedge, draw line from dart point through waistline marking. Pin dart. Machine-baste on line. Fold dart toward center; press lightly over tailor's ham.

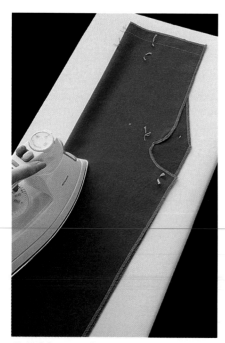

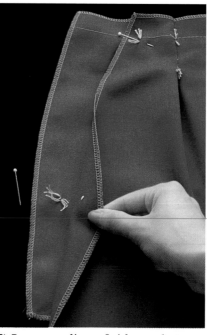

4) Fold pants front in half, matching inseam and side seam from lower edge to knee area. For creases, press lightly to crotch line of dart-fitted pants, or to waistline of pleated pants. If no crease is desired, mark foldline with hand basting.

5) Match markings of pleat, right sides together. Machine-baste pleat through markings. Press lightly in direction indicated on pattern.

6) Lap seamline of side pocket piece for slant pocket, matching markings at both ends of seamline. Machine-baste on seamline. (If side-seam pocket is included, do not attach until after first fitting.)

7) Match raw edges of right pants front and back at hemline and waistline, right sides together. Pin side seam. Repeat for left side. Machine-baste 1" (2.5 cm) side seams. Press side seams lightly, using tailor's ham in hip area.

8) Match raw edges of front and back inseam at hemline; pin to within 8" to 10" (20.5 to 25.5 cm) of crotch line. Back inseam is ¼" to ½" (6 mm to 1.3 cm) shorter than front inseam. Stretch remainder of back inseam so tailor's tacks match at crotch points; pin. Machine-baste 1" (2.5 cm) inseams; press lightly.

9) Turn one pants leg right side out, and slip it inside remaining pants leg. Pin crotch seam from raw edge at back waistline to marking at bottom of zipper opening. Machine-baste ⅝" (1.5 cm) crotch seam.

10) Press crotch seam open, from back waistline to top of curved crotch area. Press fold at center front on upper fly facing.

Perfecting the Fit

The adjustments you have made on the pattern have taken care of the majority of the changes needed. During the first fitting, you can make any minor adjustments that will improve the fit of the pants. It is helpful to have a friend assist you.

Try on the pants, pinning the center front opening along the seamline and pinning out the fullness of the pleats. Pin a piece of ¾" to 1" (2 to 2.5 cm) elastic around your waist; then pin the elastic to the pants, with the lower edge of the elastic along the seamline.

Using a full-length mirror and a large hand mirror, look carefully at the pants from all views. Refer to pages 34 to 42 for help in evaluating any fitting problems.

When adjusting the fit of the pants, first eliminate any tightness. Pants should hang from the waistline, with ease evenly distributed in the high hip, full hip, and thigh areas. If the pants bind or pull in any of these areas, you will not be able to clearly judge the fit in other areas, such as the crotch. Adjust the amount of ease as necessary.

If you have full, high hips, it may be necessary to reshape that area of the side seams to conform to your body without pulling. If the fit of the pants is too loose, adjust the side seams, making sure that the ease has been maintained. Further adjustments at the side seams may be made later (pages 83 to 85).

How to Adjust Tight or Loose Fit at Side Seams

Too tight. 1) Release fabric from side seams if center opening does not pin closed smoothly. Check for pulling or horizontal wrinkles at waist, high hip, full hip, or thigh.

2) Adjust side seams; pin with ease evenly distributed over high hip, full hip, and thigh. If pants are still tight in thigh area, crotch points may be too short (page 78) or inseams may need adjusting (page 84).

Too loose. Pin a tuck to remove any excess width at waist, hip, or thigh. Walk and sit in pin-fitted pants to check that you have not made them too tight.

Perfecting the Fit in the Crotch

Good fit in the crotch area can be difficult to achieve if you rely only on measurements. It is usually necessary to make minor changes during the fitting.

Begin by checking the crotch depth. Then adjust the crotch length at the crotch points and the waistline. Next, check to see that the crotch area of the pants follows the curve of the body; if not, reshape the crotch seamline. Even minor changes in reshaping the crotch seamline can make a smoother fit in the pants. Some crotch length is added when the crotch curve is reshaped.

Standards of Fit for Crotch

Crotch is high enough to prevent sagging, but low enough for comfort in movement.

Crotch curve of pants conforms to the crotch area of body without pulling.

How to Adjust the Crotch Depth

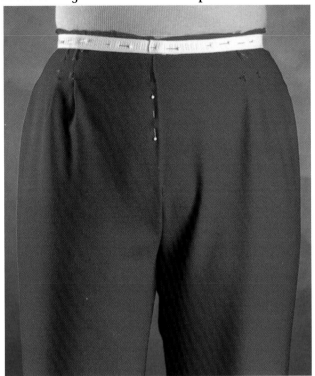

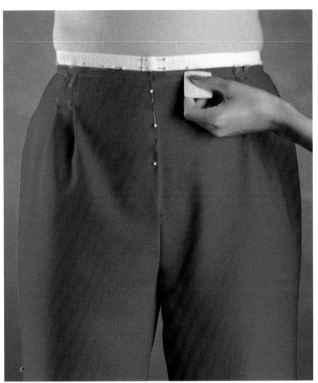

Crotch depth too short. 1) Unpin elastic at waistline if pants pull in crotch area or waistline of pants does not reach natural waistline.

2) Adjust pants for comfortable fit, allowing adequate ease in crotch area. Repin elastic with lower edge of elastic at natural waistline. Mark new seamline with chalk.

Crotch depth too long. 1) Unpin elastic at waistline if pants hang too low in crotch area or bind with body movement.

2) Adjust pants for comfortable fit, allowing adequate ease in crotch area. Repin elastic with lower edge of elastic at natural waistline. Mark new seamline with chalk.

How to Adjust the Crotch Length at the Crotch Points

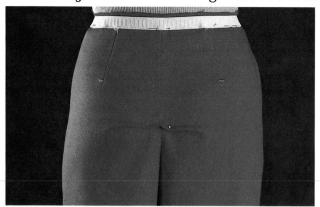

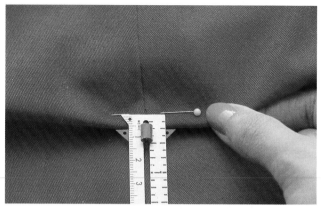

Crotch points too long. 1) Check fit. Long crotch length causes excess fabric in crotch area at center front or center back, or both. Pin tuck at center front or center back seam to determine amount of excess length to remove at crotch point; amount of adjustment may differ from front to back.

2) Measure tuck across crotch seam; double this measurement to determine amount of crotch length adjustment.

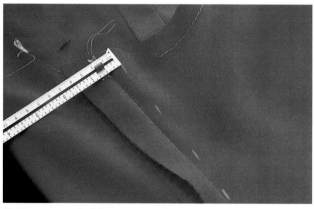

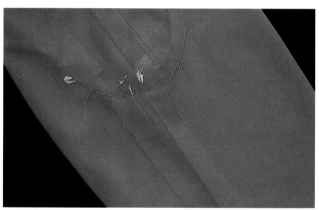

3) Remove stitching at crotch curve. Mark amount of adjustment away from inseam to shorten crotch point. Mark new seamline on inseam, tapering to knee area for a smooth line.

4) Remove stitching at inseam from crotch point to end of marking. Align front and back at inseam, matching marked seamline to original seamline. Machine-baste new inseam.

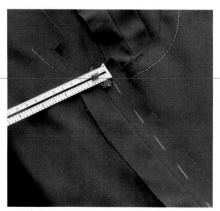

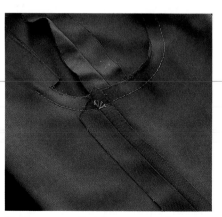

Crotch points too short. 1) Check fit. Short crotch length causes wrinkles to radiate from front crotch point, back crotch point, or both.

2) Mark ½" to ¾" (1.3 to 2 cm) from inseam to lengthen crotch point. Mark new seamline, tapering to knee area for a smooth line.

3) Remove stitching at crotch curve and at inseam from crotch point to end of marking. Align front and back at inseam, matching marked seamline to the original seamline. Machine-baste new inseam.

How to Adjust the Crotch Length at the Waistline

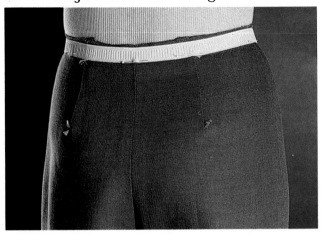

1) Check fit. If pants pull down at center front or center back, the crotch seam is too short. If there is excess fabric at center front or center back, the crotch seam is too long.

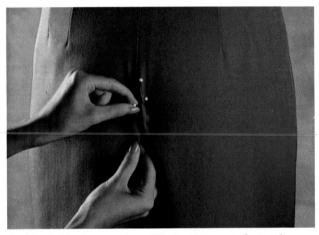

2) Repin elastic to correct the fit, raising and lowering it at center front or center back, as necessary. Mark new seamline below elastic with chalk. Transfer fitting adjustment to pattern as a wedge adjustment (page 89).

How to Reshape the Crotch Curve

1) Check fit. Excess fabric in seat area causes pulling at crotch seam. This may be indicated by diamond-shape fold below seat.

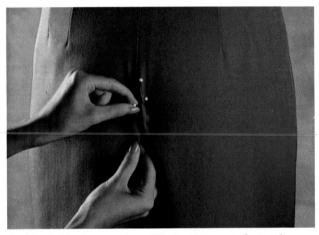

2) Pin folds from excess fabric at curve of crotch seam. Remove pants and mark deeper back crotch seamline, using the amount pinned as a guide.

3) Restitch crotch seam, tapering new seamline into front crotch curve for a smooth line, if necessary. Trim seam allowance to ⅝" (1.5 cm).

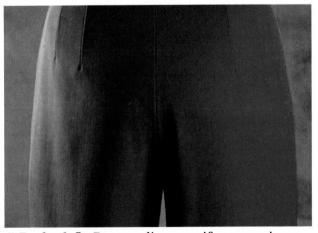

4) Recheck fit. Repeat adjustment if seat area is not smooth. Do not trim seam allowance narrower than ⅝" (1.5 cm) until crotch seam is permanently stitched.

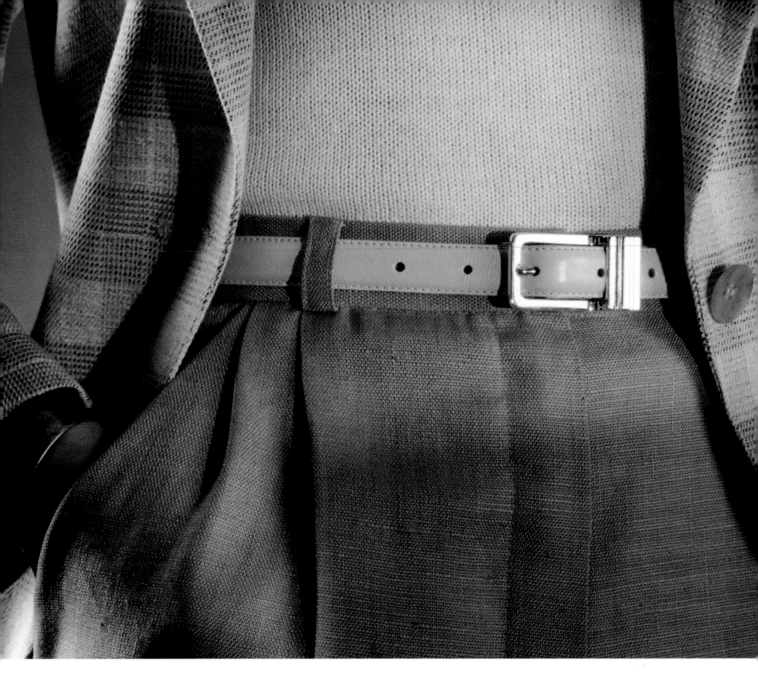

Perfecting the Fit in the Waistline & Hipline Areas

The waistline may need to be adjusted at one or both sides if you have uneven hips. To achieve a good fit in the waistline area, the pleats and darts may need to be adjusted. When adjustments are made, 1" to 1½" (2.5 to 3.8 cm) of fitting ease should be maintained at the waistline.

The amount of fullness and the angle of pleats may be changed to conform to the shape of the body. Darts may be made longer, shorter, deeper, or shallower. Or the fullness of one dart may be divided into two darts; this is especially helpful if the original dart is too deep. The new dart is usually pinned in a straight line from the raw edge to the dart point. However, the stitching line of the dart may be changed from a straight line to a slightly curved line to fit the body curves.

Standards of Fit for Waistline & Hipline

Waistline lies at natural waistline and is parallel to floor whether you are standing or sitting.

Crosswise grainline is level at the hipline.

Pleats conform to the shape of the body.

Darts lie flat against the body and point to the fullest part of hips, ending at least 1" (2.5 cm) above fullest part.

How to Adjust the Waistline for Uneven Hips

1) Unpin elastic at the waistline if grainline is not horizontal at hipline, or if pants have vertical folds at higher hip.

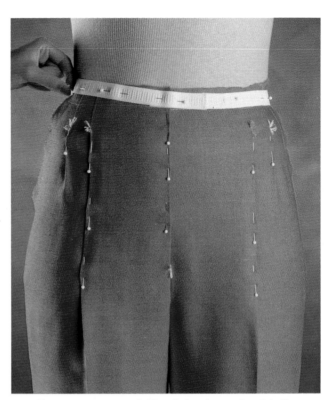

2) Adjust pants so grainline is horizontal at hipline. Repin elastic with lower edge of elastic at natural waistline. Mark new seamline with chalk.

How to Adjust the Pleats

1) Unpin elastic at waistline and release stitching from pleats if amount of fullness needs changing or if pleats pull.

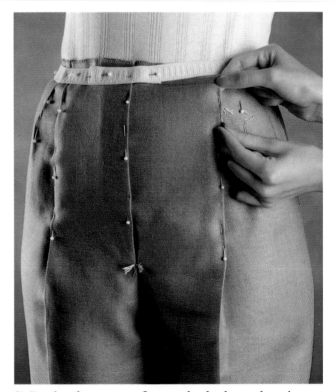

2) Repin pleats to conform to body shape, keeping outside fold of major pleat on straight of grain and aligned with center front crease line or basting line.

How to Adjust Darts

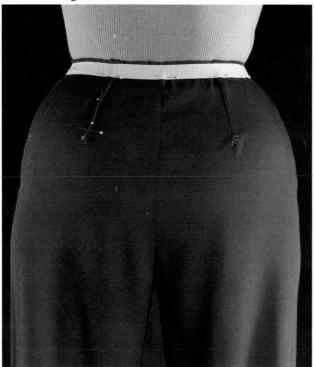

Dart too deep or too long. Remove stitching in dart if pants are tight or if fabric bubbles at dart point. Pin new dart shape shorter, shallower, or both; or make two darts, below.

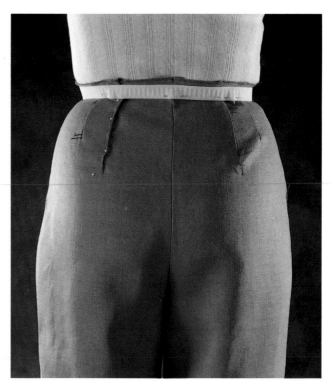

Dart too shallow or too short. Remove stitching in dart if there is excess fabric above hip area that does not fit smoothly into side seam. Pin new dart shape longer, deeper, or both.

Reshaping darts for full high hip. Remove stitching in dart if dart pulls at high hips or if there is excess fabric at waistline. Pin new dart shape, conforming to curve of high hips; or make two darts, right.

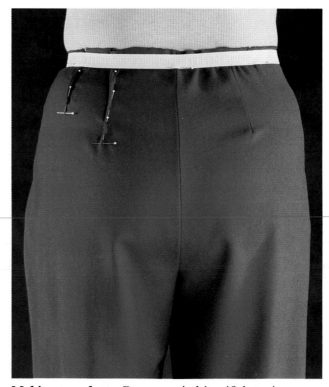

Making two darts. Remove stitching if there is pulling or excess fabric. Pin new darts, dividing fullness into two darts; dart closest to side seam is usually shorter than other dart.

Perfecting the Inseams & the Side Seams

Look closely at the way the pants legs hang. There should be equal amounts of fabric around the legs. Depending on the cut of the pants, knock-knees or large inner thighs may cause pulling at the inseam; bowlegs may cause pulling at the side seam. If there is pulling, it can be corrected by shifting the seam placement.

The side seams should hang straight from the waistline to the hemline, visually bisecting the body. At the waistline, the pants back is usually about ½" (1.3 cm) smaller than the pants front; for some figures, there may be a greater difference.

It may be necessary to remove the stitching from the side seams partway down from the waistline, or all the way to the hemline, and adjust the front and back seam allowances. This adjustment is frequently necessary if you have forward or backward hip tilt (page 33), a flat or protruding seat, or a prominent abdomen.

Standards of Fit for Inseams & Side Seams

Pants legs are balanced, with fabric evenly distributed around legs.

Side seams are straight, hang perpendicular to the floor, and visually bisect the body.

How to Adjust for Knock-knees or Full Inner Thighs

1) Check fit. Knock-knees cause pulling at inseam and diagonal wrinkles in thigh area.

2) Release stitching at side seam from hipline to lower edge. Pin or machine-baste side seam about ½" (1.3 cm) deeper from lower edge to knee line; then taper to original seamline at hipline.

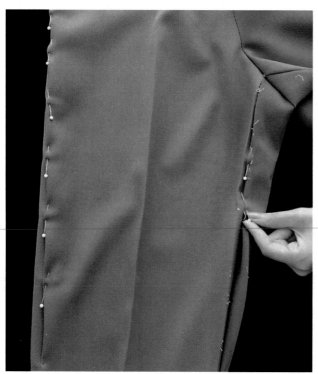

3) Release stitching at inseams from crotch point to lower edge. Pin or machine-baste inseam, letting it out an amount equal to adjustment at side seam.

4) Recheck fit. If there is still pulling in thigh area, increase the amount of adjustment up to ¾" (2 cm), and straighten seam allowance of pants back at inseam so it does not curve in the thigh area; taper adjustment for a smooth line.

How to Adjust for Bowlegs

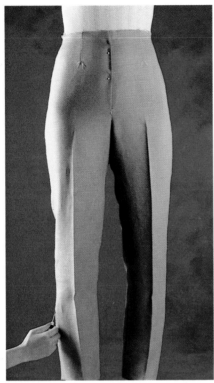

1) Check fit. Bowlegs cause pulling at side seams and diagonal wrinkles in thigh area. Release stitching at side seams from hipline to lower edge.

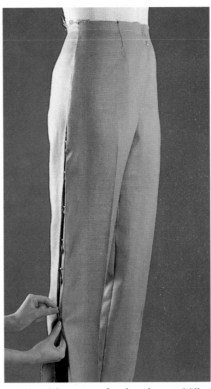

2) Pin side seam, letting it out ½" to ¾" (1.3 to 2 cm) so pants hang straight.

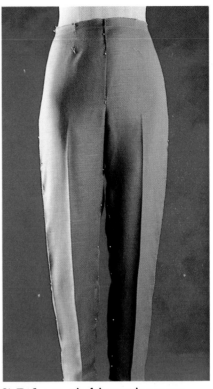

3) Release stitching at inseams from crotch point to lower edge. Pin inseam, taking it in an amount equal to adjustment at side seam.

How to Adjust the Side Seams

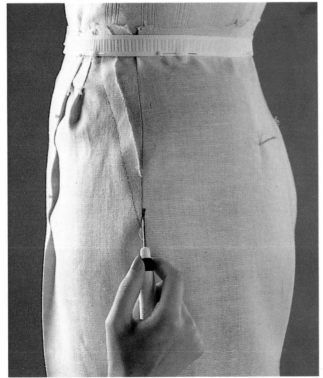

1) Release stitching on side seams if they do not hang straight or visually bisect the body.

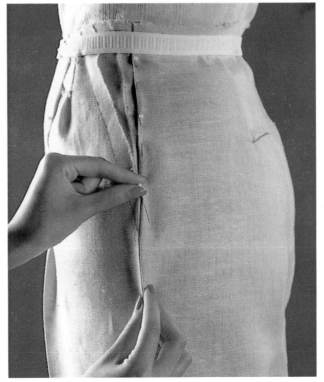

2) Fold under seam allowance as necessary to straighten seam; pin at fold. Adjust both side seams.

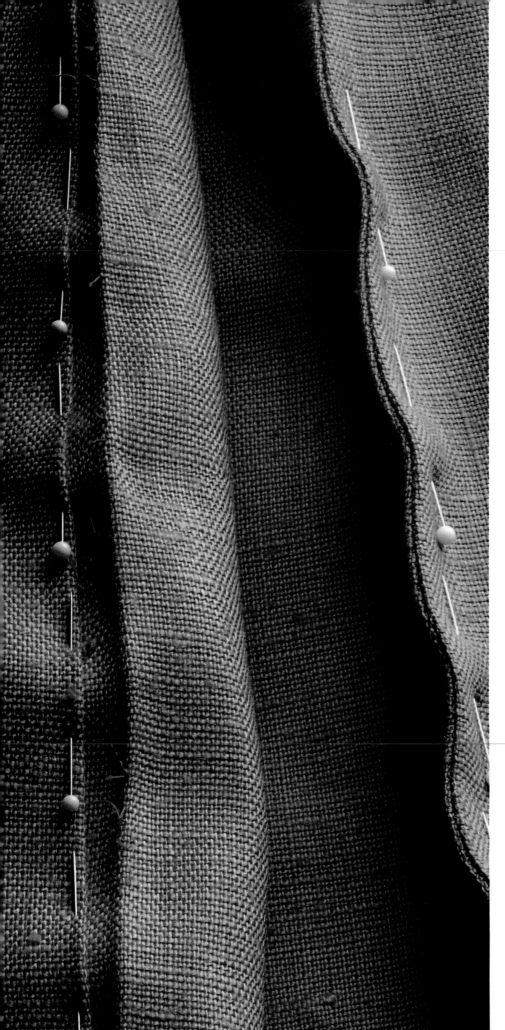

Marking Fitting Changes

Fitting adjustments marked with pins need to be marked on the inside of the garment with chalk before the seams are stitched. The method you select to mark the fitting adjustments depends on whether the adjustments were lapped or tucked.

Because it is difficult to place pins in a smooth line during the fitting, repin the adjustments accurately before marking them with chalk. When you repin seams that have been lapped, such as adjusted side seams, place the pins close to the edge of the fold. Machine-baste the seams again to check the fit.

How to Mark Lapped Seamline Adjustments

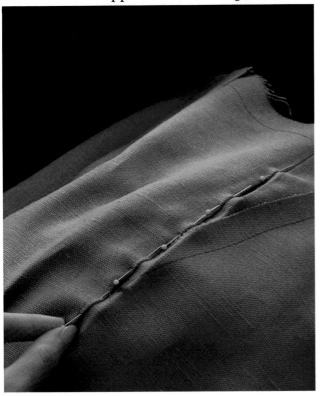

1) Repin close to folded edge, through all layers.

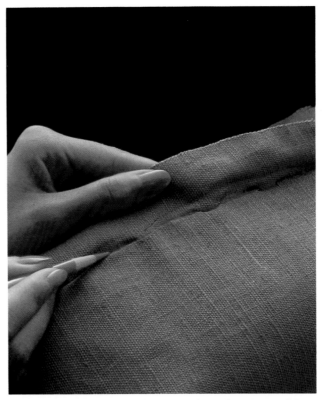

2) Turn pants wrong side out. Using pins as a guide, mark new seamline on both sides.

How to Mark Tucked Seamline and Dart Adjustments

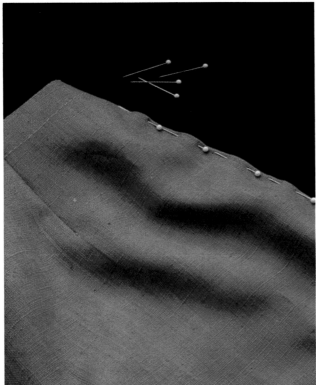

1) Adjust pins as necessary for a smooth line.

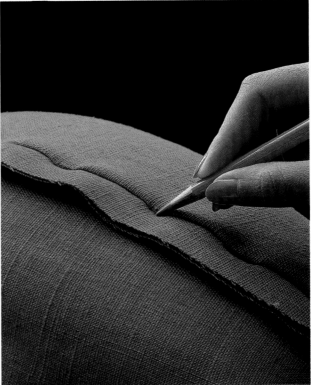

2) Turn pants wrong side out. Using pins as a guide, mark new seamline on both sides.

Transferring Adjustments to the Pattern

When fitting the machine-basted pants, you may have made additional adjustments. These adjustments are then transferred to your pattern so you will have a permanent record for future use. It may be necessary to release the basting stitches, so the pants lie flat while you transfer the adjustments.

If you have changed the position or size of darts or pleats, transfer these adjustments, using the same method as for seamlines, below.

Once the pattern changes have been transferred, erase any smudges or unused lines and finish trueing the pattern. You can then add ⅝" (1.5 cm) seam allowances to the fitted pattern, instead of the wider seam allowances that were allowed for fitting adjustments. Record all changes on the Pants Adjustment Chart (pages 30 and 31), for future reference.

How to Transfer Fitting Adjustments at Seamlines

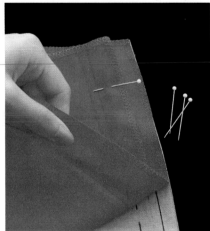

1) Align original pants seamlines to pattern seamlines, pinning as necessary.

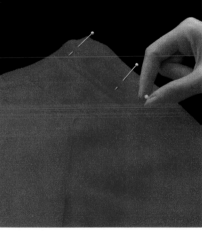

2) Use pin to make holes in pattern, about 1" (2.5 cm) apart, along new seamline.

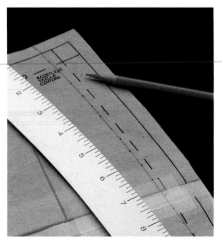

3) True new seamline, using holes as guide. Add ⅝" (1.5 cm) seam allowance.

How to Transfer Fitting Adjustments at Cutting Lines

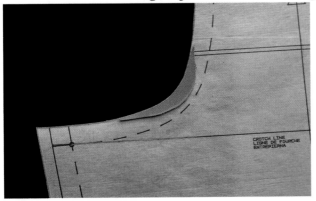

1) Place the trimmed piece of fabric on the pattern, matching original cutting lines.

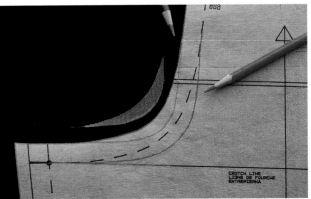

2) Mark the new cutting line; then measure and mark new stitching line. Trim excess tissue. Trim seam allowance to ⅝" (1.5 cm), if necessary.

How to Transfer Crotch Depth or Wedge Fitting Adjustments

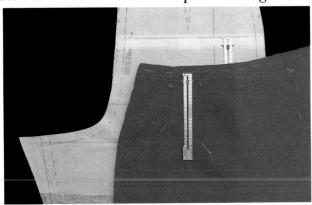

Crotch depth adjustment. Measure the amount of fitting adjustment (page 77). Make crotch depth adjustment on pattern the same amount (page 52). True seamlines; add ⅝" (1.5 cm) seam allowances.

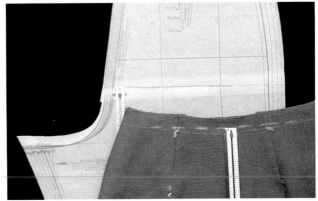

Wedge adjustment. Measure the amount of fitting adjustment (page 79) at back or front crotch seam, from original waistline to new waistline. Make wedge adjustment on pattern the same amount (pages 57 and 58). True seamlines; add ⅝" (1.5 cm) seam allowances.

How to Mark New Center Grainline

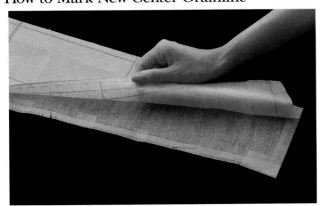

1) Fold pattern lengthwise, aligning inseam to side seam at lower edge and knee line. Crease pattern from lower edge to waistline.

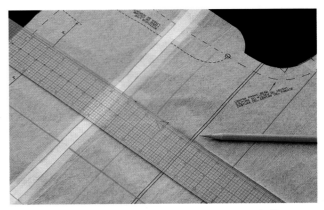

2) Lay pattern flat and draw new center grainline on crease. On pleated pants pattern, new grainline marks outside fold of major pleat; if fold of pleat does not match new grainline, adjust both pleat lines so depth of pleat does not change.

Making a Personal Fit Card

Pattern companies use their basic dart-fitted pants pattern as a guide for developing other designs. If you have fitted and used a pattern company's basic pants pattern, another pattern from that company can be fitted using the same pattern adjustments. If you fitted a pattern other than the basic pattern, the adjustments may vary somewhat, depending on the design. Each time you try a new pattern design, cut out the pants with 1" (2.5 cm) seam allowances and machine-baste the structural seams, so minor fitting adjustments can easily be made.

Keep a record, on an index card, of the adjustments you made. Refer to your Pants Adjustment Chart (pages 30 and 31), as well as to your pattern, for this information. Use this personal fit card for quick adjustments on future projects. Update the card as necessary.

Since each pattern company has a different fit, it is necessary to go through the process of fitting the basic dart-fitted pants to develop a personal fit card for each pattern company. If you like the fit from one pattern company and have adjusted that company's basic pattern, you may want to continue using designs from that company.

On your personal fit card, list the pattern company, pattern number, and date. Record any length and width adjustments needed. Note any crotch length adjustments, including wedges, crotch points, and changes in the shape of the crotch curve. Also make any other notes you think might be helpful.

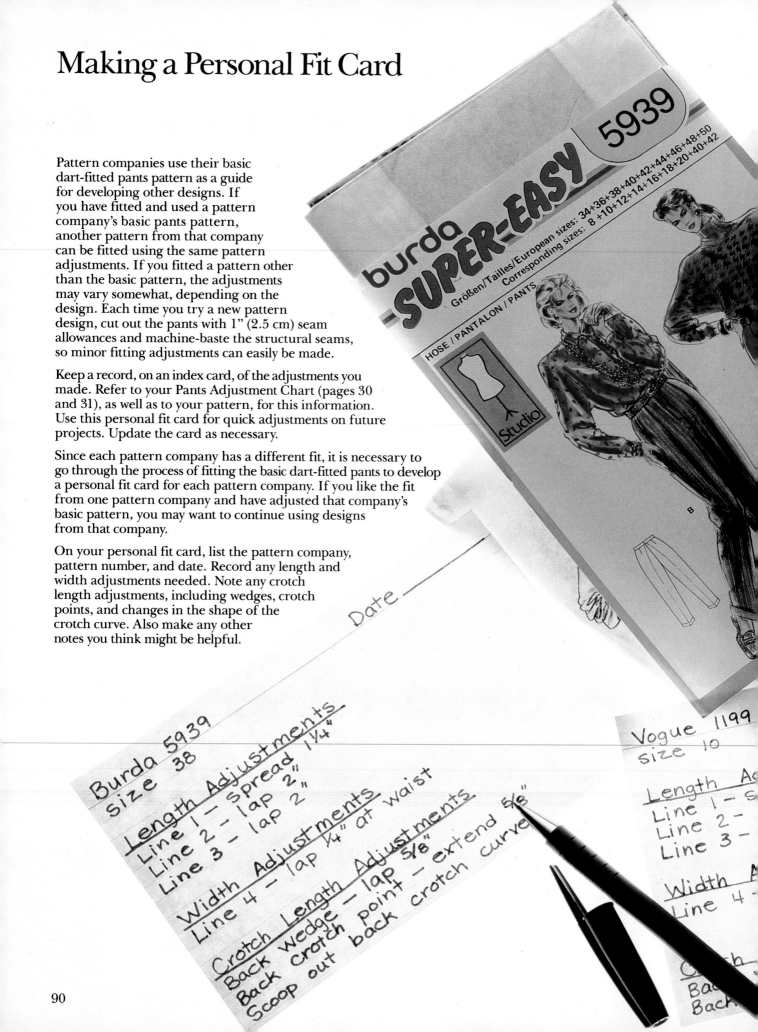

SEE REVERSE SIDE

10

Date _____

BUTTERICK
FAST&EASY

BUTTERICK® 684

SIZE/TAILLE
(6-8-10)

Butterick 6841
Size 10

Length Adjustments
Line 2 - lap 1"
Line 3 - lap 1"

Width Adjustments
Line 4 - spread 3/8" at
        spread 1/4" at

Crotch Length Adjustme
Back wedge - lap 1/2"
Back crotch points - ex
Scoop out back crotch

ments
1/4"

/8"
3/8"

ments
ad 3/8" at waist
ad 1/4" at hip

Adjustments
- lap 1/2"
point. - extend 2"

Sewing Rating/Classification-Couture
VERY EASY / TRÈS FACILE

PATTERN/PATRON

91

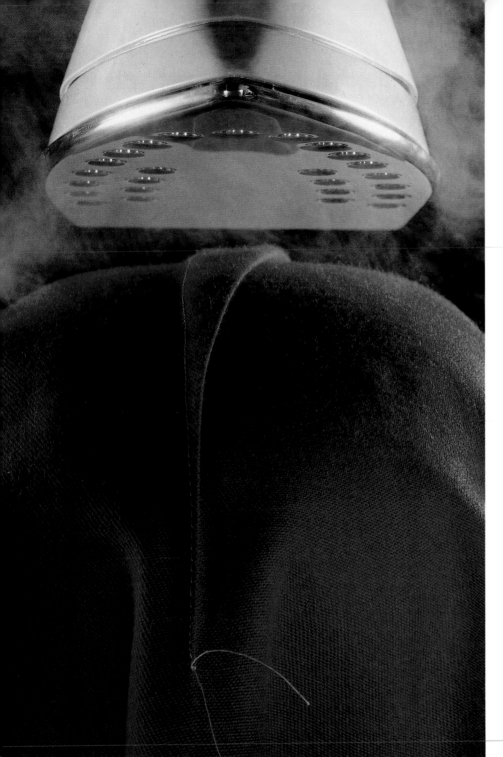

Techniques for Sewing Pants

After all the adjustments are made, the pants are ready for permanent stitching. The techniques in this section are used for sewing classic pants. Follow the pattern guide sheet if the pattern includes other design details.

Remove all but one thread in a tailor's tack before the final stitching. Remove the basting stitches in the crotch seam and in any area where a design detail, such as a slant pocket, is to be placed. If any changes were made in the seam allowances, be sure those changes are clearly marked before removing the basting stitches. The remaining basting stitches for darts, pleats, side seams, and inseams, may be left in and used as a stitching guide.

Press each seam before crossing it with another seam. Use a tailor's ham when pressing curved areas and a seam roll when pressing straight seams. A clapper, held in place until the fabric cools, will flatten the seam or dart, without overpressing.

Follow the Sequence for Sewing Pants, left. The first step after the fitting is to permanently stitch and press the darts. Follow the pattern guide sheet if pleats are to be edgestitched. If the pleats are to be released at the waistline, permanent stitching is not necessary; simply leave the basting stitches in until the waistband is applied.

Sequence for Sewing Pants

Stitch and press darts; edgestitch stitched-down pleats, if included.

Sew slant pockets, if included.

Apply fly zipper, if included.

Baste partial knee lining in pants, if included.

Stitch inseams.

Stitch side seams; stitch side seam pockets, if included.

Stitch crotch seam.

Sew lining, if included.

Apply waistband.

Apply closures on waistband.

Stitch pants hems; stitch lining hems, if included.

How to Stitch and Press Darts

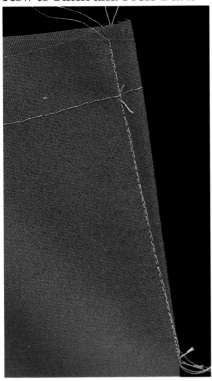

1) Stitch close to basting from wide end of dart to point, with last 4 or 5 stitches on fold; shorten stitches for 1" (2.5 cm) at wide end and ½" (1.3 cm) at point. Leave about 4" (10 cm) tails.

2) Tie knot, using pin held at point to ensure close knot. Cut thread, leaving about ½" (1.3 cm) tails.

3) Remove basting and tailor's tacks. Press dart flat on both sides to embed stitches.

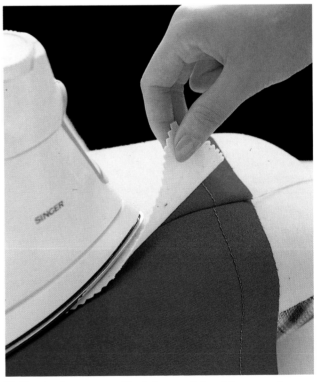

4) Place dart over tailor's ham, wrong side up, pressing dart toward center front or back. Use clapper to flatten.

5) Press dart over tailor's ham, right side up, using press cloth or iron guard to protect fabric.

Slant Pockets

Slant pockets, a standard design detail in classic pants, are formed from two pattern pieces: the pocket facing, and the side pocket piece. The pocket facing is usually cut from lining fabric to minimize bulk. A pocket stay, which is an extension of the pocket facing to the center front seam, is often included on the pattern piece. The pocket stay keeps the pockets in place and the pants smooth in front.

The finished pocket opening is slightly larger than the placement line on the side pocket piece to allow for the curve of the body. Stabilize the pocket opening to prevent it from stretching.

After you have fitted your first pair of pants and know that your pattern waistline is accurate, you may stitch slant pockets before the fitting, on other pants made from the same pattern.

How to Sew a Slant Pocket without a Pocket Stay

1) Cut stay tape or lining selvage strip length of pocket opening. Use pattern front as a guide.

2) Place pocket facing and pants front right sides together, matching pocket openings. Center stay tape over seamline on wrong side of pants front, and pin to pocket opening.

3) Stitch ⅝" (1.5 cm) seam, with stay tape on top and lining fabric next to feed dogs. Grade seam allowances.

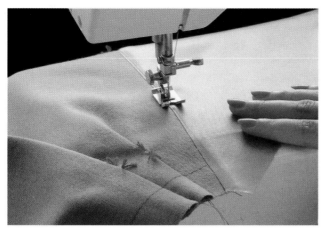

4) Press seam allowances toward pocket facing; understitch ⅛" (3 mm) from seamline.

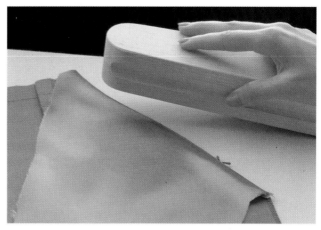

5) Fold pocket facing to inside. Steam press, using clapper to flatten edge. If desired, edge may be topstitched.

6) Place side pocket piece over tailor's ham, right side up. Position pants front over side pocket piece, matching markings and seamlines. Pin at side seam and waistline. Hand-baste pocket opening in place.

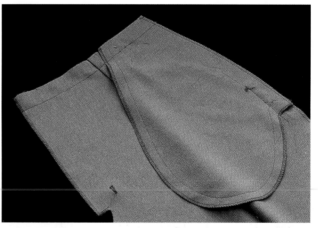

7) Pin pocket facing to side pocket piece; stitch around outer edge. Finish seam allowance. Machine-baste pocket edges at waistline and side seam.

How to Sew a Slant Pocket with a Pocket Stay

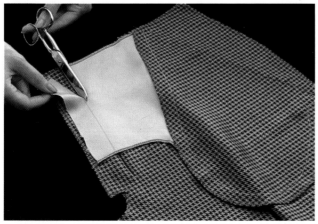

1) Follow steps 1 to 6, left. Pin pocket facing to side pocket piece; stitch around edge of side pocket piece. Trim pocket stay at center front line on overlap side of fly; do not trim stay on underlap side.

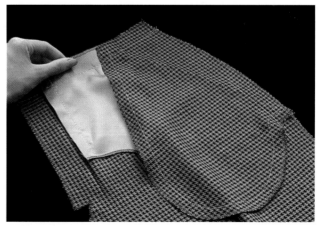

2) Machine-baste pocket edges at waistline, side seam, and ½" (1.3 cm) from center front line. Front edge of the pocket stay is caught in stitching when the zipper is applied.

Fly-front Zipper

The fly-front zipper, traditional for men's pants, is commonly used in women's pants. The fly in women's pants is usually lapped right over left. A fly shield may be added to unlined pants to prevent fabric from getting caught in the zipper.

Use a zipper 1" to 2" (2.5 to 5 cm) longer than finished zipper opening. The standard opening length is 7" (18 cm); allow up to 9" (23 cm) if more length is desired. If you have lengthened the crotch depth, you may need to shorten the zipper opening at the bottom.

For a flat method of construction, apply the zipper before stitching the pants seams. Apply lightweight fusible interfacing to the overlap fly facing to add stability to the zipper opening and help prevent zipper imprint. Interfacing extends about ¼" (6 mm) beyond center front line. For pants with pocket stay, fold back the front edge of the stay when fusing interfacing. Interfacing is especially recommended for pants made from lightweight fabrics.

How to Install a Fly-front Zipper

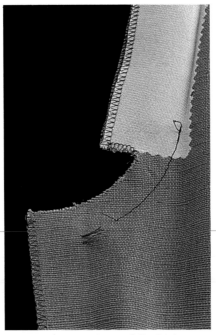

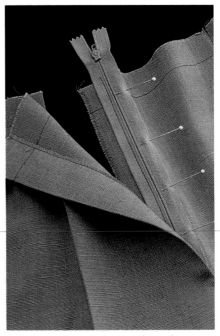

1) Cut interfacing 1¾" (4.5 cm) wide by length of fly facing, using pinking shears; fuse to wrong side of overlap facing. Cut fly shield from pants fabric 4" (10 cm) wide by length of fly facing; curve lower edge, if desired.

2) Finish raw edges of fly facings. Press fold on overlap facing at center front. Stitch front crotch seam, using short stitches, beginning about 1½" (3.8 cm) from crotch point and ending at bottom of zipper opening; backstitch 3 or 4 stitches.

3) Place closed zipper face down on underlap facing, with edge of zipper tape at center front and zipper stop ⅛" (3 mm) above bottom of zipper opening. Pin outer edge of zipper tape to facing. Using zipper foot, stitch zipper tape to facing only.

4) Fold underlap facing to wrong side; machine-baste next to foldline.

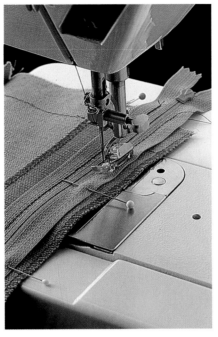

5) Match center front markings at upper edge, and pin. From wrong side, pin remaining edge of zipper tape to overlap facing only. With facing held away from pants, stitch zipper tape to facing.

6) Mark stitching line on right side of pants about 1¼" (3.2 cm) from center fold. Hand-baste next to stitching line, if desired. Stitch, backstitching 3 or 4 stitches at center fold. Remove basting. Open zipper.

7) Press fly shield in half lengthwise; finish raw edges. Place fly shield under zipper on underlap side, with upper edges matching and folded edge about 1" (2.5 cm) beyond zipper teeth. Stitch close to fold through all layers. Remove basting.

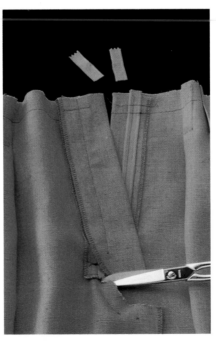

8) Staystitch, with zipper open, across both ends of zipper at upper edge; trim off excess zipper ends. Clip crotch seam allowances below the fly facing to within ¼" (6 mm) of stitching.

9) Close zipper. From wrong side, tack lower edge of fly shield to overlap facing. From right side, stitch a bar tack at lower end of zipper opening, if desired.

Seams & Creases

Stitch as close as possible to basting stitches without catching them in the permanent stitching. Remove the basting stitches before pressing the seams. A strip of stay tape or lining selvage applied along the crotch seam strengthens it and prevents stretching. Stitch the crotch curve again to reinforce the seam; then trim the crotch seam to ⅜" (1 cm) in the crotch curve for a smoother fit.

Press each seam before crossing it with another seam, using a seam roll for straight seams and a tailor's ham for curved areas. After pressing, hold a clapper in place until the fabric cools.

Pants may or may not be creased, depending on the style of the pants and your personal preference. Creases are pressed halfway between the side seam and the inseam. Press the front crease along the straight of grain, so the pants hang correctly. On dart-fitted pants, press the front crease only to the crotch line; on pleated pants, press the front crease to the main pleat. The back crease is always pressed only to the crotch line. A permanent crease may be set by dampening a press cloth with a solution of one part white vinegar and three parts water; test first on a fabric scrap for colorfastness.

How to Stitch Side Seams, Inseams, and Crotch Seam

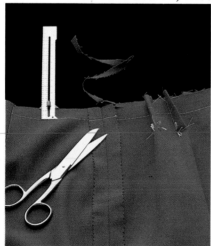

1) **Stitch** side seams and inseams, as in steps 7 and 8, page 73, using regular stitch length. Trim seam allowances to ⅝" (1.5 cm), and finish edges. Remove basting; press seams, opposite. Trim waistline seam allowance to ⅝" (1.5 cm).

2) **Pin** or baste crotch seam. Cut stay tape or narrow strip of lining selvage the length of seam; center it on seamline, and stitch from center back as close as possible to bottom of front opening.

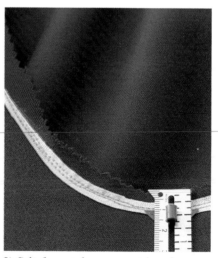

3) **Stitch** crotch curve again, close to first stitching. Trim seam allowance in crotch curve to ⅜" (1 cm), and finish edges. Press center back seam open above crotch curve, opposite.

How to Press Seams

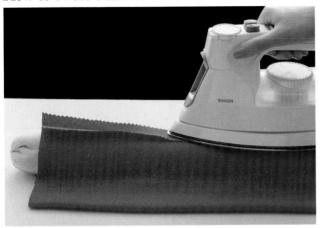

1) Remove basting. Press seam flat on both sides to embed stitches. Place straight seam wrong side up over seam roll; place curved seam over tailor's ham. Press with steam iron; use clapper.

2) Press right side up over seam roll, using press cloth or iron guard to protect fabric.

How to Press Creases in Pants Legs

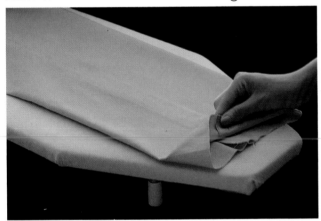

Dart-fitted pants. 1) Align inseam to side seam from lower edge to knee area, with fold on straight of grain. If front crotch point or side seam was adjusted, seamlines may not match above knee.

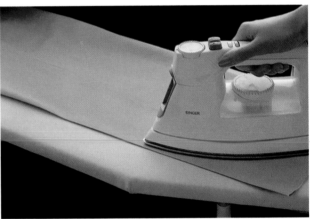

2) Press front crease from lower edge to knee area; continue pressing on straight of grain to crotch line.

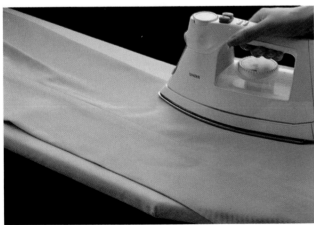

3) Press back crease from lower edge to crotch line. If back crotch point was extended, fabric may not lie flat at inseam.

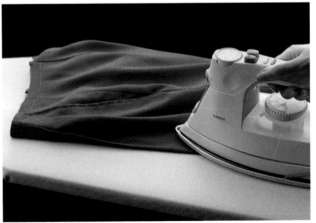

Pleated pants. Press creases as for dart-fitted pants, above, continuing front crease to waistline along straight of grain on outside fold of major pleat.

Lining Pants

Lining pants requires little time and effort and offers many advantages. Lined pants last longer than unlined pants and do not stretch out of shape. Lining also minimizes wrinkling and prevents show-through in light-colored fabrics.

Cut the lining with ⅝" (1.5 cm) seam allowances, using the adjusted pattern. Fold under the pattern at the hemline before cutting the lining; the raw edge of the lining is at the pants hemline.

If the pattern has slant pockets, pin the side pocket piece to the pattern front, with the placement line on the pocket piece aligned to the pocket opening. Use this as the front pattern piece for the lining. If the pattern has side-seam pockets, eliminate the pocket extension.

On a fly-front pattern, eliminate the fly extension, leaving a ⅝" (1.5 cm) seam allowance. If the pattern has deep pleats, you can eliminate some fullness by slashing the pattern the length of the pleat and overlapping it to make a smaller pleat.

The lining seams may be sewn on a conventional sewing machine or an overlock. The lining is attached only at the waistline, so it can be pulled out when pressing the pants.

You can line just the knee area of tapered pants to prevent bagging at the knees. This technique is especially appropriate for pull-on pants, because lining adds too much bulk at the waistline.

How to Line the Knee Area of Unlined Pants

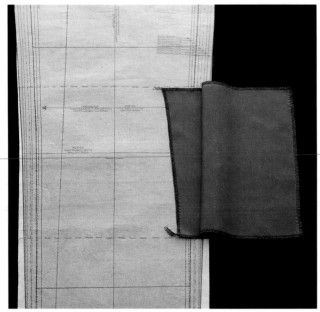

1) Mark pants front pattern 5" (12.5 cm) above and below knee line; use pattern as a guide for cutting lining the shape of pants front in knee area. Finish lining, using overlock or multistitch-zigzag.

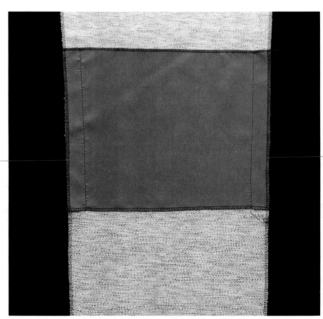

2) Lay lining on wrong side of pants front in knee area. Baste at inseam and side seam. Lining is stitched in leg seams and left free at top and bottom.

How to Line Pants with a Fly-front Closure

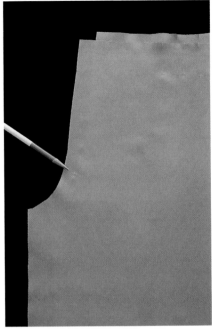

1) Cut lining, left. Mark darts, pleats, and bottom of placket opening. Match dart and pleat lines at waistline, right sides together; fold in opposite direction from those folded on pants.

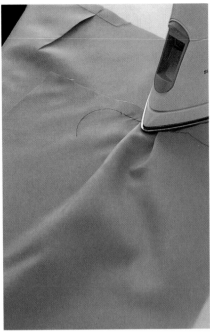

2) Baste darts and pleats at waistline. Press foldlines, leaving lower ends of pleats unpressed.

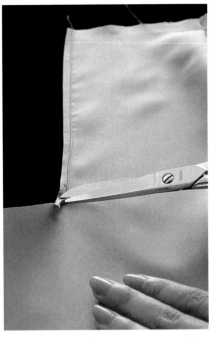

3) Press ½" (1.3 cm) to wrong side from upper edge to 1" (2.5 cm) below marking at bottom of placket opening. Turn raw edge to meet fold, and press again. Stitch close to edge of second fold. Clip below stitching.

4) Stitch side seams, inseams, and crotch seam, as in steps 7, 8, and 9, page 73, using regular stitch length; placket opening should be slightly longer than in pants. Finish seam allowances; press seam open.

5) Stitch crotch curve again over previous stitches; trim crotch curve. Finish seam allowances; press.

6) Slip lining inside pants, wrong sides together; pin at seamlines. Release stitching in pleats to align edge of lining to edge of zipper; repin pleats. Baste at waistline. Hem lining (page 111) after pants are hemmed.

Waistbands

An important part of applying the waistband is getting the proper fit. The finished length of the waistband should be ½" to 1" (1.3 to 2.5 cm) longer than your waist measurement to allow for comfort. The waistband was cut 4½" (11.5 cm) longer than your waist measurement (pages 70 and 71); the excess length will be trimmed when the waistband is applied.

Waistbands are interfaced to add stability and body. You can use a perforated fusible interfacing for easier folding at the upper edge of the waistband. Or cut a strip of fusible interfacing half the width of the waistband, or the full width, depending on the weight of the pants fabric and the interfacing.

Belt Loops

Belt loops are often added to the waistband. The finished width may vary from ⅜" to 1" (1 to 2.5 cm). Four or five belt loops may be used. If four are used, one is placed midway between the side and center seams on each front and back piece. A fifth loop may be added at the center back. Cut belt loops on the lengthwise grain of the fabric. The cut length of each belt loop is twice the finished width of the waistband. Belt loops may be applied during the construction of the waistband, as on page 107.

How to Stitch Belt Loops

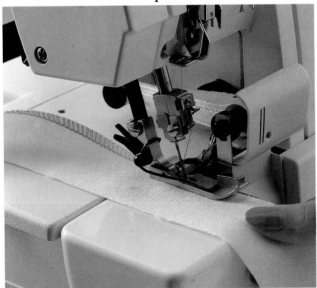

1) Cut strip of fabric 3 times finished width of belt loop; length of strip equals cut length of each belt loop times number of loops. Finish one long edge with overlock or zigzag stitch.

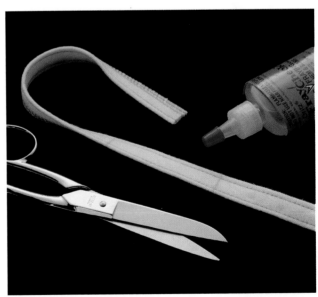

2) Fold strip lengthwise into thirds, enclosing raw edge; press. Topstitch both edges from right side ⅛" (3 mm) from fold. Mark cutting lines. Apply liquid fray preventer at marks; allow to dry. Cut strip into belt loops.

How to Apply a Waistband on Pants with a Fly Shield

1) Staystitch waistline seam. Align center front to center back seam, with zipper closed; mark folds at sides with ¼" (6 mm) clips.

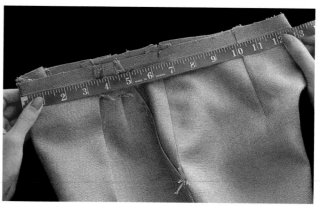

2) Refold, matching marks at sides. Measure length of waistline from center front to center back along staystitching. Double this measurement; subtract ½" (1.3 cm) to determine finished length of waistband.

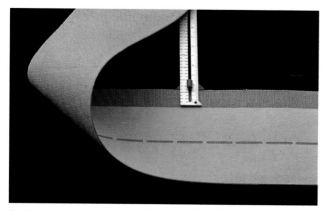

3) Fuse perforated fusible waistband interfacing to wrong side of waistband with narrowest section ⅝" (1.5 cm) from raw edge. Or use standard fusible interfacing.

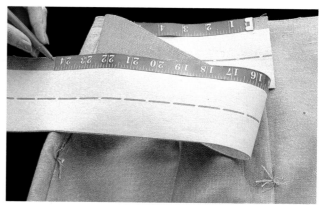

4) Place one end of waistband over center front on overlap side, with raw edges even and right sides together. Mark center front on waistband ⅝" (1.3 cm) from end. Measure from center front mark to finished length of waistband; mark center front at other end of waistband.

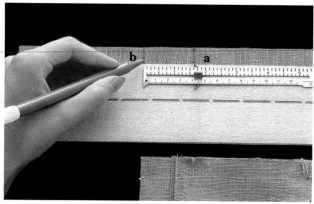

5) Mark the distance from center front (**a**) to edge of fly shield (**b**).

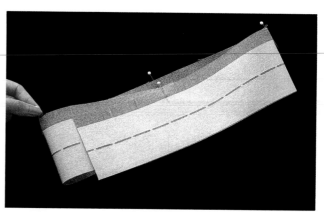

6) Match markings at center front, and mark center back at fold. Align center front to center back; mark folds halfway between, as for pants, step 1, above.

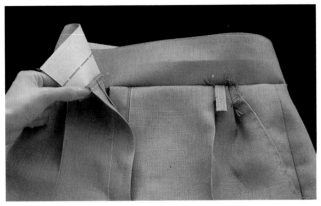

7) Baste one end of each belt loop to garment at desired position. Pin waistband to pants, right sides together, matching marks at edge of fly shield, center fronts, center back, and sides; distribute ease evenly. Stitch waistline seam. Grade seam allowances.

8) Trim excess length on underlap ⅝" (1.5 cm) beyond edge of fly shield. Press the seam allowances toward waistband. Fold waistband, right sides together; turn selvage up at ends to match waistline (arrow). Stitch ends of waistband. Grade seam allowances.

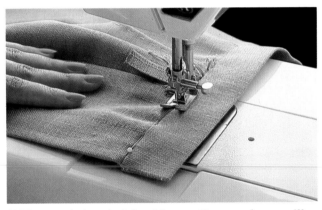

9) Turn waistband right side out. Press; selvage will extend below waistline on inside of garment. Pin in place; stitch in the ditch from right side. Topstitch, if desired.

10) Turn up belt loops, leaving ⅛" to ¼" (3 to 6 mm) slack at bottom fold. Fold under free end of each belt loop; topstitch to waistband at upper edge.

How to Apply a Waistband on Pants without a Fly Shield

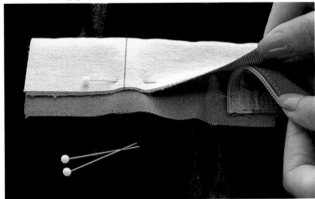

1) Follow steps 1 to 4, left. Mark underlap end of waistband 2" (5 cm) beyond zipper teeth. Follow steps 6 and 7, left. Tuck pants into waistband at underlap end.

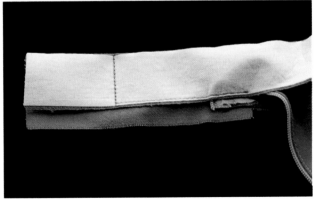

2) Stitch across end and lower edge of underlap; continue stitching over previous stitches, through all layers, to center front marking. Trim excess on underlap. Follow steps 9 and 10, above, to finish pants.

Closures

All pants need two closures, a main closure and a secondary closure, to distribute the stress and to prevent pulling at the top of the zipper. When positioning the secondary closure, hold the waistband closed, duplicating the slight curve of the body.

For dress pants, select closures that are flat and thin. A flat button or a wide hook and eye works well for the main closure. A medium or large snap is a good choice for a secondary closure, but a hook and eye or a button may be used. Types of closures may be combined on the same pants. For example, a button may be used for the main closure, and a snap for the secondary closure.

Apply the closures with a double strand of thread, using beeswax to prevent tangling of threads.

How to Sew the Main Closure (button and buttonhole)

1) Stitch horizontal buttonhole near overlap end of waistband. Mark button placement under buttonhole.

2) Stitch button on right side of underlap, making a thread shank. For extra security, back the button with a smaller, flat button on wrong side.

How to Sew the Secondary Closure (button and buttonhole)

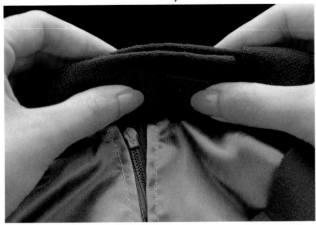

1) Stitch horizontal buttonhole near underlap end of waistband. Hold waistband closed and slightly curved to determine placement of button.

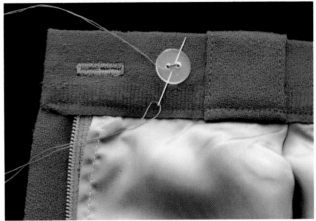

2) Stitch flat button on wrong side of waistband so stitches do not show through to right side, making a short thread shank.

How to Sew the Main Closure (hook and eye)

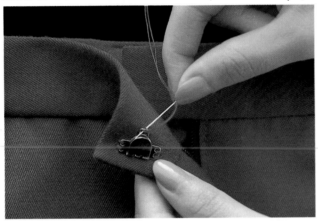

1) Place hook on wrong side of overlap end of waistband. Stitch in place with short, close stitches so stitches do not show through to right side.

2) Position eye under hook; stitch in place with short, close stitches.

How to Sew the Secondary Closure (snap or hook and eye)

1) Mark end of underlap with pin on wrong side of waistband. Stitch ball half of snap or hook to wrong side of waistband near waistline seam, within marked area, so stitches do not show through to right side.

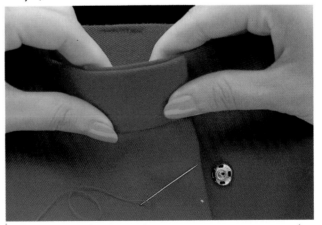

2) Hold waistband closed and slightly curved to determine placement of socket portion of snap or eye. Stitch securely in place.

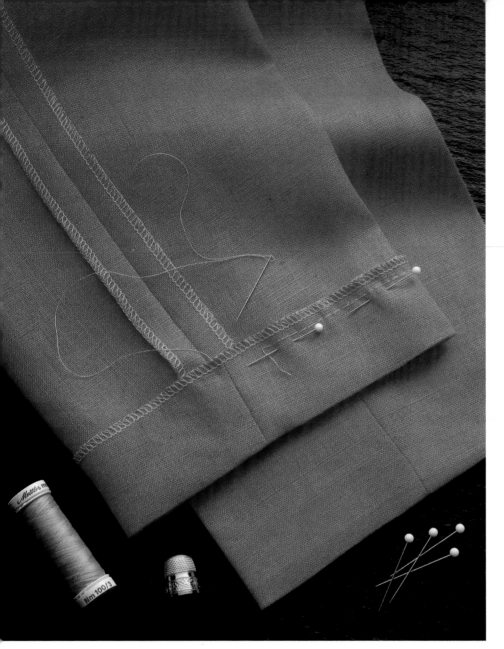

Hemming Pants

To ensure that the pants length is accurate, the pants legs are pinned up and hemmed after the waistband is applied. When pinning the hemline, wear the shoes you intend to wear with the pants. The length of the pants varies with the style of the pants and the width of the pants leg.

For classic pants, the hemline should skim the foot or shoe in the front and extend to the top of the heel in the back. Hemlines may be parallel to the floor, or they may be ½" (1.3 cm) longer in the back than in the front.

If the hemline angles in the back, the hem allowance is clipped at the center front to allow the hem to lie flat when stitched, and the excess fullness in the back of the pants leg is eased.

The standard hem allowance for pants is 2" (5 cm), but for lightweight fabric, the hem depth may be trimmed to 1" to 1½" (2.5 to 3.5 cm).

When making pants with cuffs, it is important to adjust the pattern to the correct length. Pants with cuffs are hemmed parallel to the floor.

How to Hem Pants with Straight Hemlines

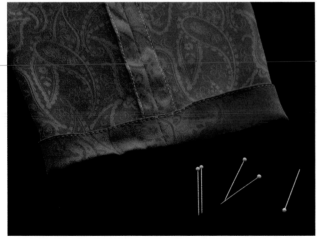

1) Turn up and press hem lightly, checking to see that it lies flat. Trim hem depth evenly. Finish raw edge, if necessary; firmly woven fabrics may be pinked.

2) Pin hem in place. Turn back upper edge of hem ¼" (6 mm) and stitch to pants by hand, or machine-blindstitch. Tack hem securely at both seams.

How to Hem Pants with Angled Hemlines

1) Turn up hem; press lightly. Trim hem depth evenly. Finish raw edge, if necessary. Clip hem about ½" (1.3 cm) at center front; spread hem to fit pants leg.

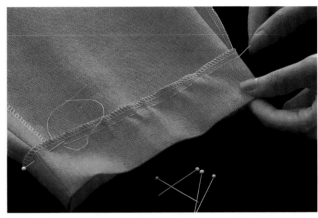

2) Ease excess fullness in back with basting stitches. Stitch hem as in step 2, opposite.

How to Hem Pants Lining

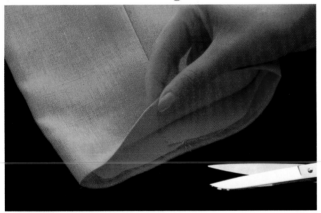

1) Hem pants as for straight hemlines, opposite, or as for angled hemlines, above. Trim lining to finished length of pants.

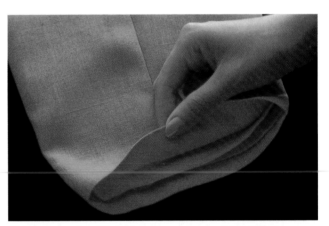

2) Turn under 1" (2.5 cm) to wrong side of lining, and press fold. Turn under raw edge to meet fold, and press again. Machine-stitch close to edge of second fold.

How to Hem Pants with Cuffs

1) Mark cuff foldlines with tailor's tacks. Finish hem edge; turn up hem, matching markings. Hand-baste along hemline. Press foldline on lower edge.

2) Turn lower edge to right side to form cuff; fold and press along hemline. Fold cuff down; stitch hem by machine or by hand.

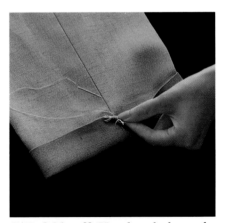

3) Refold cuff. Hand-tack through all layers at seamlines about ¼" (6 mm) from upper edge of cuff. Press crease in cuff, if pants are to be creased.

Design
Variations

Simple Design Changes

You may want to sew different styles of pants after fitting the basic, or classic, pants pattern. Instead of purchasing and fitting another pattern, you can often make changes on the basic pattern. Even small changes, such as adding a watch pocket at the waistline, can give the pants a different look.

Or you may want to use flat pattern methods to change the leg width or add pleats. To keep the basic pattern for future use, copy it, using tracing paper, before making these changes; trace the seamlines, darts, pleats, and grainline. Add seam allowances after the

desired changes are made on the pattern, following the guidelines on page 66.

Watch Pocket

The watch pocket is a popular design detail. It can be used to tuck away small items or to add design interest to pants. It can be added at a horizontal seam, usually at the waistline or yoke seam. The pocket edge may be curved, straight, or angular. For a flat method of construction, a watch pocket may be added before the pants seams are stitched.

How to Add a Watch Pocket

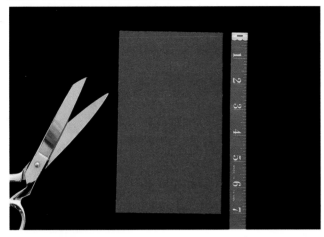

1) Cut 7" × 4" (18 × 10 cm) pocket piece from pants fabric; contrasting color may be used, if desired. These measurements include ⅝" (1.5 cm) seam allowances.

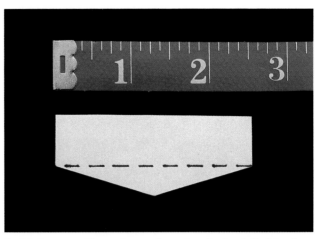

2) Make a cardboard template the desired finished shape of pocket edge, with opening 2½" (6.5 cm) wide; add ⅝" (1.5 cm) waistline seam allowance.

3) Center template on wrong side of one short end of pocket piece. Mark stitching line.

4) Place marked edge of pocket piece at desired location on pants, right sides together. Stitch on marked line, using short stitch length.

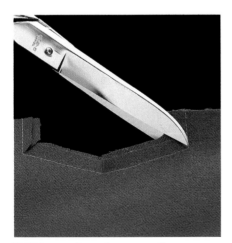

5) Trim and grade seam allowances. Clip, as necessary.

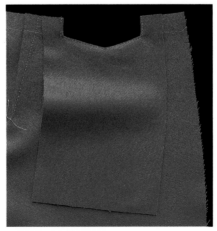

6) Turn pocket piece to inside. Press, using clapper to flatten the edge. Edgestitch or understitch opening.

7) Fold pocket piece up, matching raw edges; pin and stitch. Finish seam allowances. Machine-baste at waistline.

Adding Pleats to a Pattern

A pattern that has small pleats may be changed, using flat pattern methods, so the major pleat is deeper. The pattern is cut lengthwise, and spread to provide the extra fullness for the major pleat, tapering the fullness to the hemline.

To change a dart-fitted pants pattern into a pleated pants pattern, taper the fullness of the major pleat to the hemline. The fullness for the second pleat is spread only to the hipline.

The amount of fullness created by the pleats may vary, depending on personal preference. Decide how deep you want each pleat; usually the pleat on the grainline is deeper than the second pleat. Then determine the amount of fabric taken up by the pleats, sometimes called pleat space. This space equals the combined width of the original pleats or darts plus the amount the pattern is spread. To make two pleats, divide the pleat space between the two.

How to Increase the Depth of the Major Pleat on a Pattern

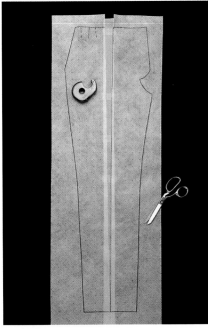

1) Mark the center grainline on pattern (page 89). Cut on marked line to, but not through, hemline. Spread pattern the desired amount for major pleat.

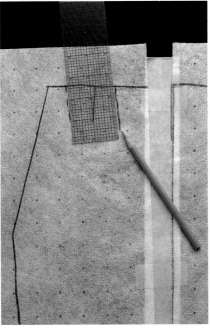

2) Mark placement line for outside fold of major pleat on center grainline; mark other pleat line so depth of pleat takes up original pleat space plus amount spread.

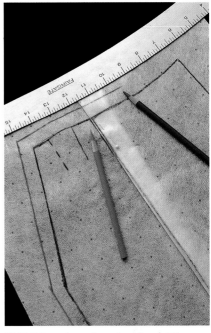

3) Fold major pleat in place. True waistline. Add seam allowances.

How to Change a Dart-fitted Pattern to a Pleated Pattern

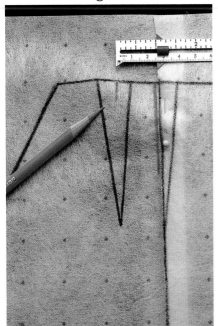

1) Follow step 1, above. Mark pleat placement line for outside fold on center grainline; mark other pleat line so pleat takes up original dart space plus amount spread. Fold pleat in place. Mark a line for second pleat 1" (2.5 cm) away from major pleat toward side seamline.

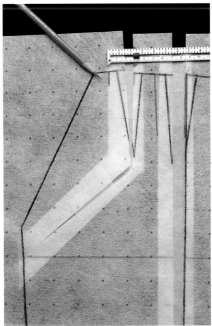

2) Unfold major pleat; cut pattern on marked line 4" (10 cm) down from waistline and diagonally to, but not through, hipline at side seamline. Spread pattern up to ¾" (2 cm). Mark pleat lines for second pleat.

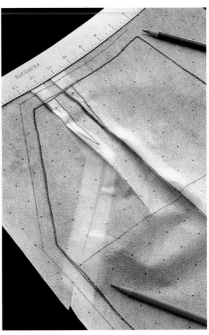

3) Fold both pleats in place. True waistline and side seamline. Add seam allowances.

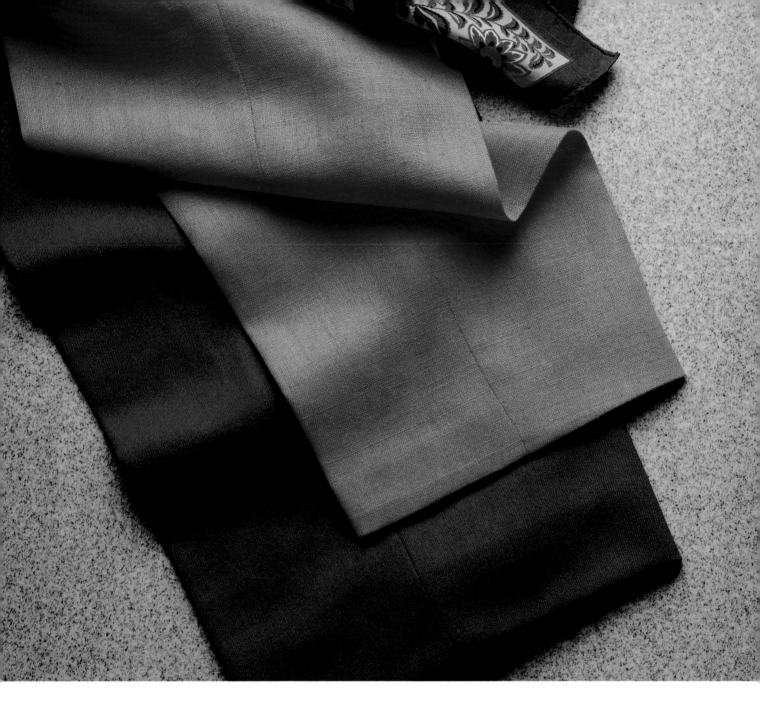

Leg Width Variations

A simple flat pattern method can be used to change the width of the pants legs, making them wider or narrower than the original pattern. Leg width adjustment may also be desirable to retain the original design after making a hip width adjustment (pages 54 and 55).

When changing the width of the pants legs to a narrow width, be sure the pants leg will fit over the foot when the toe is pointed. Add a placket or slit at the hemline, if necessary. Pants legs can be made narrower on knit fabrics that stretch than they can on woven fabrics.

Determine the difference between the original width of the pattern and the new width desired; divide this

difference evenly between the inseams and side seamlines, so the grainline will not be distorted and the pants will hang properly.

The new seamlines are drawn in a smooth line from the hemline, tapering to the original seamline partway up the pants leg. The amount of change required and the style of the pattern determine how high the seamlines need to be blended in order to draw a smooth line. If the change is great enough to be blended above the knee area, blend the seamline farther up on the side seamline than on the inseam, with equal width distributed at the knee line. After changing the width of the pants leg, add the seam and hem allowances to the pattern.

Guidelines for Changing the Width of Pants Legs

New side seamline can be drawn from the lower edge to any point between the knee line and the hipline, depending on the style of the pants and the amount of fullness desired in the thigh area.

New inseam can be drawn from the lower edge to any point between the knee line and the crotch point, depending on the style of the pants and the amount of fullness desired in the thigh area.

Distribute the amount of change evenly between side seam and inseam below the knee line. The side seam may be blended higher than the inseam above the knee line.

How to Change the Width of Pants Legs

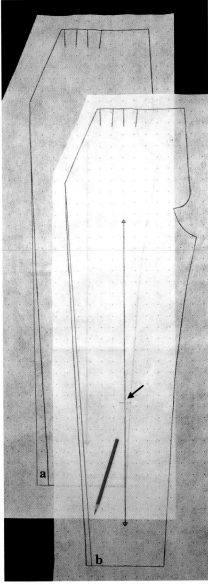

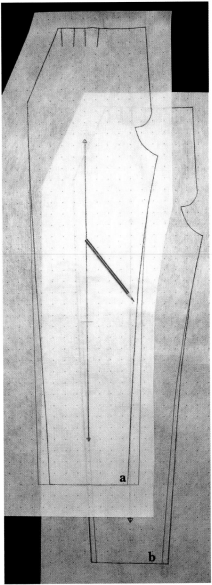

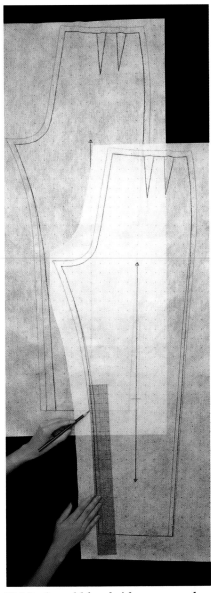

1) Mark knee line on pattern (arrow). Mark ¼ total amount of change desired along hemline at pattern front side seamline to increase **(a)** or decrease **(b)** width. Draw new seamline from mark at hemline to original seamline, blending the line as in guidelines, above.

2) Mark the same amount of change at hemline and knee line of inseam as marked on side seamline to increase **(a)** or decrease **(b)** width. Draw new seamline, blending the line as in guidelines, above.

3) Mark and blend side seam and inseam on pattern back to the same points as on pattern front. Add seam and hem allowances.

Adding Cuffs

You can change the look of the basic pants by adding cuffs. A cuff detail must be added to the pattern before cutting out the pants. Extra length is added to both the front and back pattern pieces, and the seamlines at the cuffs are shaped to match the tapered pants legs.

The depth of the cuff is usually about 1½" (3.8 cm), but may vary from 1¼" to 2" (3.2 to 5 cm). Determine the finished length of the pants before adding the cuff, using your fitted basic pattern as a guide.

How to Add Cuffs to a Pattern

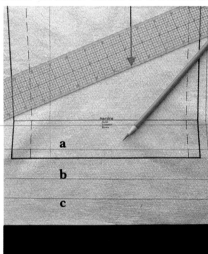

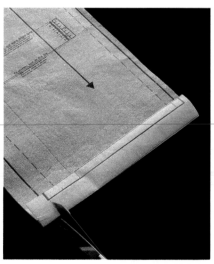

1) Measure desired finished depth of cuff below hemline; draw foldline **(a)**. Draw second foldline **(b)** the same depth away from first foldline. Mark new hem edge **(c)** ½" (1.3 cm) narrower than cuff depth.

2) Trim pattern at new hem edge. Fold pattern on foldline **(a)**, wrong sides together; then turn up cuff on foldline **(b)**.

3) Extend cutting lines, and trim pattern before unfolding. Mark the seamlines.

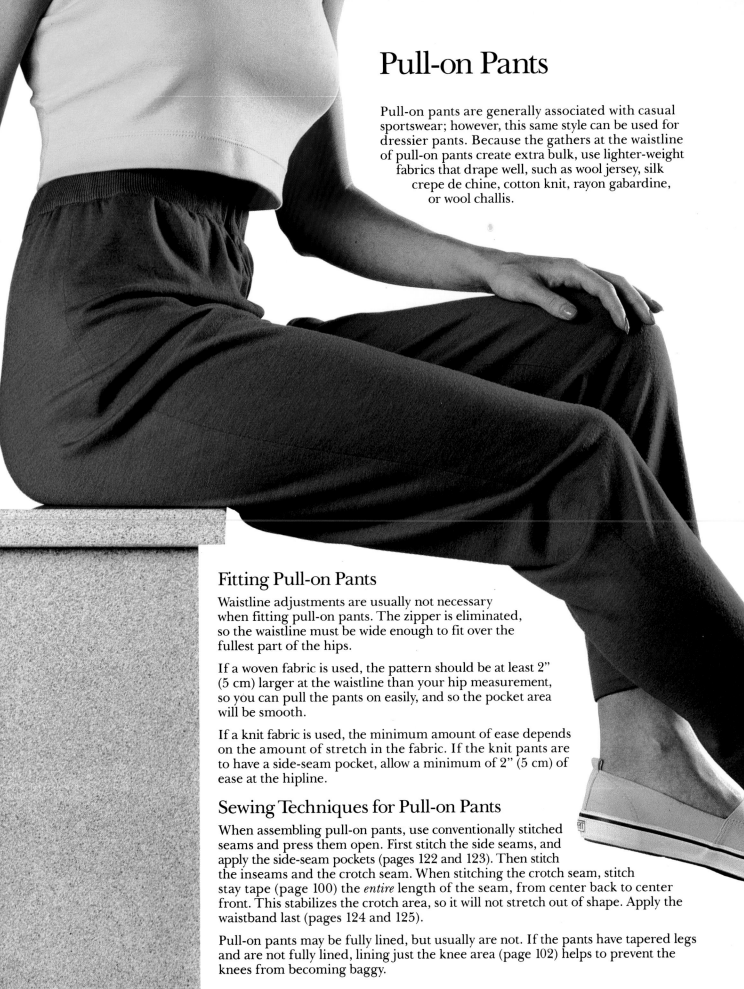

Pull-on Pants

Pull-on pants are generally associated with casual sportswear; however, this same style can be used for dressier pants. Because the gathers at the waistline of pull-on pants create extra bulk, use lighter-weight fabrics that drape well, such as wool jersey, silk crepe de chine, cotton knit, rayon gabardine, or wool challis.

Fitting Pull-on Pants

Waistline adjustments are usually not necessary when fitting pull-on pants. The zipper is eliminated, so the waistline must be wide enough to fit over the fullest part of the hips.

If a woven fabric is used, the pattern should be at least 2" (5 cm) larger at the waistline than your hip measurement, so you can pull the pants on easily, and so the pocket area will be smooth.

If a knit fabric is used, the minimum amount of ease depends on the amount of stretch in the fabric. If the knit pants are to have a side-seam pocket, allow a minimum of 2" (5 cm) of ease at the hipline.

Sewing Techniques for Pull-on Pants

When assembling pull-on pants, use conventionally stitched seams and press them open. First stitch the side seams, and apply the side-seam pockets (pages 122 and 123). Then stitch the inseams and the crotch seam. When stitching the crotch seam, stitch stay tape (page 100) the *entire* length of the seam, from center back to center front. This stabilizes the crotch area, so it will not stretch out of shape. Apply the waistband last (pages 124 and 125).

Pull-on pants may be fully lined, but usually are not. If the pants have tapered legs and are not fully lined, lining just the knee area (page 102) helps to prevent the knees from becoming baggy.

121

One-piece Pocket for Pull-on Pants

A one-piece pocket that is stitched directly to the pants reduces bulk. The stitching also becomes a design detail, and extra design interest is created by centering the pocket on the side seam. This type of pocket is appropriate for pants that are not closely fitted, such as pull-on pants.

If a woven fabric is used, finish the seam allowances before applying the pocket. The directions, below, allow ⅝" (1.5 cm) seam allowances at the waistline and side seams. The pocket opening should be stabilized so it will not stretch out of shape.

How to Sew a One-piece Pocket

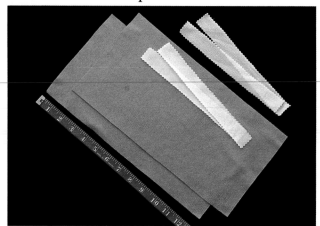

1) Cut two 7" × 13" (18 × 33 cm) pocket pieces from pants fabric on lengthwise grain. Cut four 1" × 8½" (2.5 × 21.8 cm) strips from lightweight fusible knit interfacing on lengthwise grain, using pinking shears.

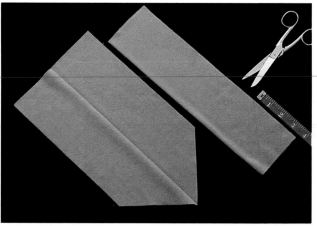

2) Fold pocket pieces lengthwise, wrong sides together. Press crease lightly. Measure 3½" (9 cm) from one end on raw edge. Cut a diagonal line from this point to the center fold to shape lower end of pocket. Finish raw edges, if necessary.

3) Place fusible interfacing on wrong side of pants at pocket opening, with raw edges even and with one end 1" (2.5 cm) lower than upper edge. Fuse in place.

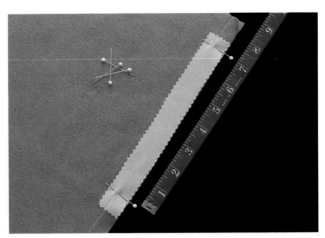

4) Mark 7" (18 cm) pocket opening, beginning 1½" (3.8 cm) from upper edge. Stitch side seam, leaving pocket opening unstitched. Finish seam allowances, if necessary.

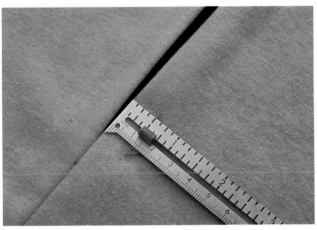

5) Press side seam open, including pocket seam allowances. On right side, mark topstitching pivot points at lower end of pocket opening, ½" (1.3 cm) on either side of opening and ½" (1.3 cm) below opening.

6) Topstitch ½" (1.3 cm) from pocket opening, starting at upper edge and pivoting at marks, as shown.

7) Position center crease of pocket piece under pocket opening, right sides up. Pin in place. From wrong side, machine-baste ¼" (6 mm) from outside edge of pocket piece.

8) Topstitch from right side, using basting stitches as a guide; pivot at corners and side seamline. Remove basting threads. Repeat for second pocket.

Waistband for Pull-on Pants

The elasticized waistband for pull-on pants has a slightly shirred appearance for a soft effect. Nonroll elastic is inserted after the waistband is applied. The width of the waistband is determined by the width of the elastic. The elastic may be 1" to 3" (2.5 to 7.5 cm) wide, but 1½" to 2" (3.8 to 5 cm) elastic is usually preferred.

To reduce bulk at the waistline, the waistband is cut only 1½" (3.8 cm) longer than the hip measurement,

and the waistline of the pants is gathered to fit the waistband.

When woven fabric is used, cut the waistband on the lengthwise grain, with one edge of the waistband along the selvage. When knit fabric is used, cut the waistband on the crosswise grain. To further reduce bulk at the waistline, the edge of the waistband is not turned under on the wrong side of the pants.

How to Attach a Waistband for Pull-on Pants

1) Cut waistband from woven fabric along selvage, with length equal to hip measurement plus 1½" (3.8 cm), and width of waistband twice the width of elastic plus 1¼" (3.2 cm). Stitch short ends, right sides together, in ¼" (6 mm) seam; press open.

2) Stitch two rows of gathering stitches in waistline seam allowance of pants, if pants are larger than waistband. Divide pants into fourths, matching center front and center back and pin-marking folds at sides. Divide waistband into fourths; pin-mark.

3) Place waistband and pants, right sides together, with waistband seam at center back. Match markings, and pin. Pull up gathering stitches to fit; pin.

4) Stitch waistband to pants, using ⅝" (1.5 cm) seam allowance; grade. Press seam allowance toward waistband.

5) Fold waistband to width of elastic plus ⅛" (3 mm); press fold. Pin other edge of waistband in place from right side. Stitch in the ditch, leaving 2" (5 cm) opening at center back.

6) Cut the elastic equal to waist measurement. Insert elastic with a bodkin. Lap ends of elastic and secure with safety pin. Try on pants, and adjust elastic if necessary.

7) Stitch ends of elastic securely, using multistitch-zigzag. Stitch opening closed. Stitch in the ditch at center back seam to secure elastic; stitch at sides, if desired.

Index